here and now

HERE AND NOW

an approach to writing through perception

FRED MORGAN

Merced College

HARCOURT, BRACE & WORLD, INC.

New York / Chicago / San Francisco / Atlanta

to my mother

Florence H. Morgan

— a dedicated teacher

ISBN: 0-15-535620-8

Library of Congress Catalog Card Number: 68–20727

Printed in the United States of America

Contents

Preface ix

introduction

Observing 1
Showing 2
Limiting 3
Giving Specifics 5

1

perceiving objects

Class Exercise 7
Writing Assignment 8
Sketching Assignment 10
"A Study of Two Pears," Wallace Stevens 11
PLATE I: *Still Life,* Willem Kalf 13

2

perceiving the immediate environment

Class Exercise 15
Writing Assignment 16

"Big Two-Hearted River: Part II," Ernest Hemingway 17
Class Writing Exercise 25
Sketching Assignment 26
"The Great Figure," William Carlos Williams 27
PLATE II: *I Saw the Figure 5 in Gold,* Charles Demuth 29

3

perceiving emotional attitudes

Writing Assignment 32
Class Writing Exercise 33
"Arrangement in Black and White," Dorothy Parker 33
"Snake," D. H. Lawrence 37
PLATE III: *Reservoir,* Robert Rauschenberg 41

4

perceiving thoughts

Writing Assignment 44
Class Writing Exercise 44
"The Second Tree from the Corner," E. B. White 45
"A Dream of Fair Women," Kingsley Amis 50
PLATE IV: *Blind Bird,* Morris Graves 53

5

extending awareness

Class Exercise 56
Writing Assignment 56
Class Writing Exercise 56
"The Death of Colonel Freeleigh," Ray Bradbury 57
"Morning Song" from *Senlin,* Conrad Aiken 62
PLATE V: *The Starry Night,* Vincent van Gogh 65

6

observing a person

Class Exercise 71
Writing Assignment 71
Class Writing Exercise 72
from *The Ram in the Thicket,* Wright Morris 72
"Ex-Basketball Player," John Updike 79
PLATE VI: *American Gothic,* Grant Wood 81

7

evaluating possessions

Writing Assignment 84
Class Writing Exercise 84
"My Wood," E. M. Forster 85
"Salutation," Ezra Pound 89
PLATE VII: *The Money Changer and His Wife,* Marinus van Roijmerswaele 91

8

evaluating a person

Class Discussion 93
Writing Assignment 94
Sketching Assignment 94
Class Writing Exercise 94
"The Witness," Katherine Anne Porter 95
"Innocence," Thom Gunn 98
PLATE VIII: *Heilige Nacht,* George Grosz 101

9

identifying with a person

Class Exercise 103
Writing Assignment 104
Class Writing Exercise 104
"Sonny's Blues," James Baldwin 105
"Mr. Flood's Party," Edwin Arlington Robinson 132
PLATE IX: *The Prisoner,* Francisco Goya 135

10

looking at a custom

Class Discussion 138
Writing Assignment 138
Class Writing Exercise 138
"A & P," John Updike 139
"Tract," William Carlos Williams 145
PLATE X: *The Kiss,* Constantin Brancusi 149

11

examining a goal

Class Discussion 152
Writing Assignment 152

Class Writing Exercise 153
from *Invisible Man,* Ralph Ellison 154
"The Unknown Citizen," W. H. Auden 167
PLATE XI: *Government Bureau,* George Tooker 169

12

looking at an institution

Class Discussion 172
Writing Assignment 172
Class Writing Exercise 173
Alternate Exercise 173
"The Human Factory," Alfred Kazin 173
"The Death of the Ball Turret Gunner," Randall Jarrell 179
PLATE XII: *Echo of a Scream,* David Alfaro Siqueiros 181

13

reliving a past experience

Class Discussion 184
Writing Assignment 184
Class Writing Exercise 184
"Memories of a Missouri Farm," Mark Twain 185
"Grinding Scythe," Robert P. Tristram Coffin 194
PLATE XIII: *Family Tree,* Aaron Bohrod 199

14

searching for meaning

Class Discussion 202
Writing Assignment 202
Class Writing Exercise 202
"A Mother's Tale," James Agee 203
"Was a Man," Philip Booth 221
PLATE XIV: *Girl Before a Mirror,* Pablo Picasso 223

Index of Authors and Titles 225

Index of Artists and Plates 227

Preface

Here and Now is a book of fourteen units designed to improve the student's writing by developing his perception. Each unit is built around a particular area of perception or point of view and consists of assignments, illustrations (prose readings, poems, and works of art), and discussion questions. The instructor may use the units in the order in which they are presented at the pace of one a week or in any way they function best for his students.

The book is based on the premise that good writing grows organically out of good thinking and that good thinking must begin with the materials of immediate experience. Accurate and well-integrated perception of the self and of the environment is primary. Lack of such perception results in reliance upon stereotypes and clichés and in the absence of specifics.

In the assignments the student is asked to examine systematically the specifics of his own experience. The prose readings, poems, and works of art with their accompanying questions then show him how similar perceptions can be expanded and interpreted; it is hoped that these examples will lead him toward increasingly complex and interesting experiences of his own. In each case, the illustrations have been chosen to show expansions and variations of the unit theme rather than simply to illustrate that theme. The illustrations have been placed after the assignments for two reasons: first, to let more emphasis fall upon the creative than upon the interpretive processes; and second, to provide, through the assignments, some analogous experiences that promote the student's involvement in the material.

Here and Now also incorporates an integrated series of exercises in organization; however, since the chief business of this book is to provide the meaning, not the means, these are limited to the simplest principles of exposition. It is expected that many instructors will use *Here and Now* in conjunction with a handbook of writing fundamentals.

Parts of the assignments in Units 2, 3, and 4 have been very loosely adapted from ideas in the popular *Gestalt Therapy* by Frederick Perls, Ralph Hefferline, and Paul Goodman, and I wish to give these authors credit for their inspiration without holding them responsible for the outcome. I would like to express my warmest thanks for the germinal suggestions and the encouraging example of Dr. Charles W. Scott Hope of San Francisco State College, who first showed me the path that led to this book; and for the generous assistance of May Grant Robbie, chairman of the Language Arts Division of Merced College.

FRED MORGAN

here and now

introduction

observing

The first step in improving your writing is to improve your observing. Probably, like most of us, you do not observe the things and people around you — or yourself — as well as you could. You may take too much for granted and reflect the observations and opinions of others; perhaps you write in ready-made generalities instead of reflecting yourself and your environment. A person whose eyesight or hearing is faulty may not be aware of his difficulty until he tests his faculties. Just as some people go for years without discovering that one of their senses is impaired, most people probably go through life with underdeveloped powers of observation. Right now, try a few simple tests of your observation.

Choose a tree that you pass by every day or one in your own yard. Do you really know what it looks like? See if you can draw an accurate picture of it on a piece of paper. How thick is the trunk? How does it taper? How far up do the branches begin, and how are they related to the trunk? Do they occur in groups, or are they spaced out in a random way? What shapes are they? What shapes are the leaves or needles?

Now try the same thing with a coin. Without looking at it, draw a picture of the head of a penny or a dime, putting the portrait and the lettering in what you think are the right places. Though you need not expect to draw a recognizable portrait, you should know which way the men face and how much of their clothing appears. Now look at the real coin. And, the next time you have a chance, look at the real tree you tried to draw.

These are tests of your visual observation. Close your eyes for a minute and try the other senses. Can you hear clearly, in your mind, the voice of a person very close to you, such as your mother or father? Can you recreate the smell of a baking cake or the taste of butter? Can you feel in your hand the sensation of stroking a particular cat or dog, the coolness of a knife handle? Can you feel in your body the sensation of running with your eyes closed, or must you *see* yourself running?

These small experiments may convince you that you are not perfectly in contact with your environment. Most people are not. But then, most people are not good writers, either, or good thinkers — or even very good "livers." And everyone can learn to live better, think better, and write better.

Good writing stems from good observation, poor writing from poor observation.

showing

The following is an unsuccessful student essay. See if you can determine why it is not good writing.

A MEMORABLE EXPERIENCE

Our trip to Disneyland last year was an experience I will never forget.

The morning of the great day finally arrived. We all got up bright and early and had breakfast. Then we all worked at getting our things together and packed the car. At nine o'clock we left, with great feelings of anticipation in our hearts. The weather was fine, and we all had a wonderful time while traveling. At last we arrived at Disneyland.

After we bought our tickets, we rode the monorail all around Disneyland, craning our necks to see the hundreds of wonderful sights below and all around us. It was one of the most thrilling experiences I ever had, and I was sorry when it was all over.

But there were even better things to come. For example, we took a spectacular boat ride down a primitive jungle river and saw many interesting animals on the way. It was just like being in Africa. We also visited a realistic western frontier town, where we saw just how people used to live in the Old West. From this experience I gained a lot of knowledge of American history. We had many other experiences like this which were fascinating and educational, and I felt that my visit to Disneyland was one of the most valuable experiences I have ever had.

Tired but happy, we all piled into our car and started the long trek home. On the way we had dinner at a good restaurant which we all enjoyed, and when we got home I headed straight for bed and sweet dreams of Disneyland.

Does the writer tell you anything about Disneyland that you could not find in advertisements and travel brochures? Does he tell you anything about the trip that would make it seem different from anyone else's trip to Disneyland?

The writer says that the trip was an experience he will never forget; yet he writes as though he had forgotten almost everything about it. His essay could very easily have been written by someone who had never been to Disneyland.

Who are the members of the writer's family? He does not even let us know how many there are. What time of year did they go? We have no hint of what the weather was like except that it was "fine." What does he mean, "we all had a wonderful time while traveling"? We know nothing of what they did or saw.

Go through the essay, sentence by sentence, asking yourself questions the writer does not answer.

Nearly all the evidence that would back up the writer's general statements is, of course, missing. Especially lacking is evidence of what the experience was like and what the people having the experience were like. The writer has *told* us some things, though not enough; he has not *shown* us anything.

Show more than you *tell.*

Showing means rolling in the movie camera — a camera that not only sees and hears but smells, tastes, and feels as well. It means using your senses and writing down what you see, hear, smell, taste, and feel. It means taking a word like "breakfast" and letting us taste and smell the sausage and eggs and coffee. It means letting the reader share your experience with you instead of telling him your conclusions about it.

limiting

But, you may say, if the writer showed us the whole trip in detail, he would have to write a hundred pages! And so he would. What should he have done, then?

He should have *limited* his subject to a small part of the experience that he could have covered well. The monorail trip alone would have been plenty to write about, or the boat ride, or the frontier town.

Let us assume that the writer had chosen what might seem to be one of the dullest parts of the experience, starting the trip in the morning. If he had *limited* the subject to that alone, had *observed* well, and had determined to *show* us more than he *told* us of what happened, he might have come out with something like this:

A MEMORABLE EXPERIENCE

Getting my eight-year-old brother, Ronnie, ready to go on a trip is always a memorable experience. He is the nonconformist in our family and usually has his own ideas. I remember especially well the morning last June when we had the problem of getting Ronnie ready to go to Disneyland with us.

First, of course, I had to get Ronnie out of bed. At a quarter past seven, with the smell of frying sausage already making my stomach growl, I padded up the stairs in my pajamas and pounded on his door. No response. I shoved the door open against its barricade of soiled clothes, toy cars, roller skates, and plastic guns, holding my breath against the odors of dirty socks, decaying cookie crumbs, and model-airplane glue. Under the covers was a shapeless lump, very much like a turtle defending itself inside its shell. Knowing it to be dangerous, I pinned its arms first and then shook it thoroughly. It snarled, hissed, struggled, and finally surrendered.

Getting Ronnie into the tub was no problem; he was too sleepy to know what was happening. But getting him out was another matter. After fifteen minutes of yelling at him, I finally burst into the bathroom to find him lying on his back, completely submerged, using one of our father's best pipes for a snorkel. (This episode cured my father of carelessly leaving his pipes in the bathroom.) Once I had dragged Ronnie's ears above the surface, a little propaganda about the pancakes cooling on his plate was enough to get him going.

My troubles were not over, however. After we had finished breakfast and Dad had the old Dodge warmed up, Ronnie was nowhere to be found. Dad called him in his best foghorn bass, Mother screamed threats in her most hysterical soprano, and I added my piercing two-finger whistle, but the only result was that old Mr. Picard across the street slammed down his window. Naturally, I was the one delegated to find Ronnie. I searched the entire house. I peered under his bed and into his closet, finding my long-lost baseball mitt and three unopened cans of tennis balls but no Ronnie. I searched the attic, the entire downstairs, and the back yard. Just as I was returning down the front steps, I heard a suspicious little rustle under the house. On my hands and knees, peering into the musty dark, I saw a light blur that seemed to move.

"Is that you, Ronnie?"

"Sh-h-h! Don't scare him," came an irritable whisper from the darkness.

"*Now* what do you think you're doing?" I shouted, losing my patience.

"I was catching Felix, but you spoiled it," he pouted, scrambling toward me. "He wants to go with us." Felix is our pure-bred alley cat.

It was useless to explain that running under the house wasn't Felix' way of telling us he wanted to go to Disneyland. I just grabbed Ronnie, took him inside, and cleaned him up again. This time I kept his scrawny little neck firmly in my grip until I had him safely in the car.

The purpose of this essay is the same as that of the first one: to communicate an experience. But this one communicates *more* about *less,* and that is one of the reasons it is better. Another reason is that it is full of *specifics.* It *shows* the reader what the experience was like.

giving specifics

One kind of poor writing is writing that is too *general*. Good writing makes some generalizations but supports them with plenty of *specifics*.

A *general* statement is true of many instances, as in "Most cats don't like to ride in cars." We do not know whether a general statement is true or not until we have observed a number of specific examples.

A *specific* statement tells what has actually been observed, as "My old gray alley cat, Felix, ran under the house when my little brother tried to put him in the car." Several specific observations such as this might convince us that the generalization "Most cats don't like to ride in cars" is true. A good writer convinces his reader by giving him plenty of specifics on which to base his own judgment.

Some general statements can never be proved because they are expressions of feeling. They are called *opinions*. An example of an opinion might be, "Cats make the best pets." "Best" is an opinion word. No one can prove to you that cats are the best pets; you may just happen to like alligators.

Although opinions can never be proved, they can be supported with evidence designed to win the reader over to your way of thinking. The first essay we read does not convince us that the writer's trip to Disneyland was a memorable experience, but the second essay does convince us that getting Ronnie ready to go on a trip is a memorable experience. The writer convinces us by letting us experience the specifics of one episode. He gives us sights and sounds and smells, and he tells us facts. He could have omitted the first paragraph – in which the only generalizations he makes occur – without damaging the essay or weakening his point.

Good writing, then, contains good evidence accurately observed and clearly presented.

Does good writing also consist of well-chosen words, clear sentences, and coherent paragraphs? Yes, indeed. But you will find that when you know what you want to say, and when you have learned to write in concrete terms, your expression will begin to improve.

The first step is to improve your powers of observation. The following assignments are designed to increase your perception of things around you and of yourself in your environment.

Drawing by Cork in the *Saturday Review*

1

perceiving objects

> People earnestly seek what they do not want, while they neglect the real blessings in their possession – I mean the innocent gratification of their senses, which is all we can properly call our own.
> —*Mary Wortley Montagu*

class exercise

Examine a penny. Looking at it as though you had never seen it before, try to describe it so that, say, an English-speaking Martian who had never seen a coin could draw a clear picture of it. Your instructor may wish to try to draw on the board what he sees in your words. Here are some things to remember when describing:

1. Give the parts of your description in reasonable order. First, the person to whom you are communicating must know the general size, shape, and color of the object. Then he must be told the more conspicuous details. Last, he must be given the small details. *Go from large to small.* Imagine yourself drawing a sketch: you would not start with details.
2. Give enough information. It is not sufficient, for example, to say, "It says 'In God We Trust' at the top." Where are the letters, exactly? What kind of letters are they? Script, old English, block letters? How large are they? How are they made visible against their background?
3. Use all your senses. Don't just look at the penny; smell it, taste it, rub it between your fingers, estimate its weight, ring it against something, test its hardness with a fingernail and a knife blade.

4. Try to find the best words. What makes the head of the man stand out against the background? It is not a picture, since it is not painted or drawn; it is not engraved, for that would mean that it was cut into the surface. Probably the best word is "embossed." If this is not in your vocabulary, try "in relief" or, at least, "raised above the surface."
5. Use analogy. Often there are no words to describe certain shapes, colors, and other qualities. An *analogy* is a comparison with some other similar thing familiar to your reader. What is the rim of the penny *like?*

Now, if there is time, describe a common wooden pencil in the same way you have described the penny.

writing assignment

Describe a lemon. (An orange, apple, or egg may be substituted if you do not have a lemon in the house.)

1. First, inspect the lemon closely. Observe its shape, color, texture, weight, hardness, smell, taste. Jot down all your observations as you make them, until you have an exhaustive list of qualities.
2. Experiment with the lemon in all the ways you can think of. Treat it as though it were a laboratory specimen, continuing to use all your senses. Describe the results of each process, making a second list of observations.
3. Now rewrite all of your observations, putting them into a logical sequence.
4. Write your report on the lemon, showing your reader completely and clearly what you have found out. Let him know everything about what a lemon is like, as though he had never seen one. Use analogy where it is useful to make a shape or quality clear. What is the smell of the peeling like? Of the juice? What is the organization of the inside like? Strive to make such things perfectly clear.

The following is a successful student description of the kind you have been asked to write. Test your description against this one of a kitchen match.

THE MATCH

The kitchen match I have in my hand is a stick of light-colored wood about two and one-half inches long and an eighth of an inch thick. The wood is soft and has been finished roughly so that small slivers curl up from the surfaces and corners here and there.

About one fourth of an inch at one end of the stick has been pinched – as though some sort of machine had been used to grip it – in such a way that the corners are flattened, making the end of the stick nearly round. At the other end of the stick a lump of red grainy material is attached. This lump is shaped much like an avocado, with the end of the stick thrust into the stem end of the fruit. The lump is only slightly larger in diameter than the stick. The edges of the lump which overlap the stick have an uneven, flowing appearance, as though the grainy solid had once been a liquid into which the stick was dipped. The last sixteenth of an inch of this lump, the part which would be the blossom end of the avocado, consists of a white cap of material similar to the rest of the lump except for its color. When examined closely, the surfaces of both the red and the white parts are seen to sparkle with minute, glittering grains like fine sand.

The wood of the stick smells like fir or spruce. It has a slightly unnatural taste, as though it had been chemically treated. The lump at the end is heavier than the wood, so that when the stick is dropped it falls lump first and hits with the white cap down. The lump seems to have no distinct taste; however, when it is dampened, it emits an acid smell. When the stick falls on a hard surface, the sound of contact is a sharp "clink," almost musical, indicating that the wood is dry in spite of its softness. When the stick is broken between the fingers, the sharp snap it makes confirms this. In addition, it breaks in such a biased way as to indicate that the length of the stick does not exactly correspond with the grain of the wood.

When the white cap is scratched vigorously against a rough surface, it suddenly bursts into nearly white flame with a loud crack. Immediately the white cap turns black and ignites the red portion of the lump, which burns rapidly back toward the stick with a large yellow flame, hissing and smoking slightly with a strong, acrid smell. The burning of the red portion is less vigorous than that of the white but strong enough to force tongues of flame outward and downward as well as upward. It is consumed in about two seconds, during which the stick itself is ignited. The lump is now entirely black and somewhat larger than before, and the flame reduces itself from a flaring burst about two inches high to a steady triangle about an inch high as it travels slowly along the length of the stick, pushing ahead of it a ring of clear liquid which seems to sweat out of the wood. The triangle is bright yellow flame except at the base, where it is transparent, and along the bottom beneath the stick, where it is a distinct blue color. Occasionally the apex of the triangle wavers and extends itself upward into a long thread of darker orange flame which becomes a thin streamer of black smoke. The only sound at this time is an intermittent crackling together with a very faint hissing or boiling sound. The acrid smell has been replaced by the smell of burning wood.

As the flame moves back along it, the stick first browns, then blackens, glows bright red, shrinks to half its original thickness, curls, and finally blackens again, emitting a stream of white smoke. In its final form, after the flame has passed, the stick is black, shiny, and curled upward with small wrinkles or bumps along its top edge, and it has become so brittle that it easily crumbles into black powder when it is touched. If it is handled carefully, the swollen head of harder black material will remain attached, and the entire object will be a shrunken and twisted replica of what it was before the burning. If it is dropped gently an inch or so onto a hard surface, it will make a brittle, high-pitched metallic sound, and if it is broken it will snap off quickly and cleanly. Its smell now is the familiar smell of wood ashes. If the head is crumbled carefully and the texture of the different parts observed, it can be discovered that the stick originally extended through the lump of red grainy material to the base of the white cap.

sketching assignment

This is an on-the-spot description assignment that asks you to sketch with words the same way an art student sketches with his charcoal or pencil. If conditions permit, it may be done during the class period, and your instructor may wish to look over your shoulder now and then to make suggestions, just as an art teacher does.

Select a tree. Describe it as rapidly as you can, following the same kind of order you used in describing the lemon. Give the general outlines; then indicate first the details that distinguish it from other kinds of trees and then those that distinguish it from other individual trees of the same kind. Try to describe your tree so that your reader could distinguish it from a number of similar trees.

If there are no trees near your school, use a building.

A Study of Two Pears

WALLACE STEVENS

I

Opusculum paedagogum.*
The pears are not viols,
Nudes or bottles.
They resemble nothing else.

II

They are yellow forms
Composed of curves
Bulging toward the base.
They are touched red.

III

They are not flat surfaces
Having curved outlines.
They are round
Tapering toward the top.

IV

In the way they are modelled
There are bits of blue.
A hard dry leaf hangs
From the stem.

V

The yellow glistens.
It glistens with various yellows,
Citrons, oranges and greens
Flowering over the skin.

VI

The shadows of the pears
are blobs on the green cloth.
The pears are not seen
As the observer wills.

---

* A small instructive work.

1. Why does Stevens feel it necessary to say that the pears "are not flat surfaces/Having curved outlines"?
2. Are pears in any way like viols, nudes, or bottles? How are they different? Why does Stevens say they are not like these things?
3. Does Stevens use any of the senses other than sight?
4. What do you think the purpose of the poem is? What does the poem do for the reader?
5. Has Stevens observed the pears well? What could you add from your own observations of pears?

---

1. What qualities of the objects he paints is Kalf especially interested in? Does he attempt to call up sensations from any of the senses other than sight? Which ones?
2. Stevens says, "The pears are not seen/As the observer wills." Is Kalf trying to see objects in his own way? How do his painted objects differ from real objects?
3. What do you think Stevens' comment on this painting might be?
4. Why has Kalf painted a peeled lemon rather than an unpeeled one?
5. A great deal of work and skill went into this painting. What do you think its purpose is? Why would a person buy such a picture?

PLATE I

STILL LIFE: Willem Kalf The Hague, Mauritshuis

Drawing by Russell Brockbank in *The Brockbank Omnibus,* Perpetua Books, London, 1957

2

perceiving the immediate environment

The tragedy of life is not so much what men suffer, but rather what they miss.
—*Thomas Carlyle*

The human mind is not like a suitcase. It will not burst from being overfilled. It is more like the computer in which new circuits are set up to deal with each new piece of information; the more circuits it has, the more problems can be answered. The more creative and resourceful a person is, the more contact he has with the many things going on around him. Nothing is irrelevant. The mind's capacity to absorb the chaos of experience and to make sense of it is almost infinite. One definition of intelligence is the ability to observe and to make connections among observations.

As you go through the day, remind yourself every now and then to notice something you have not noticed before. Look for something you have not really seen: an object, a shadow, a color, a texture. Make yourself aware of smells, of the feel of things, of temperature, of the sensations within your body. Slow down for a minute while you are eating and taste your food. Work at being in contact with your environment.

class exercise

Relax and let your senses turn on. Close your eyes occasionally to let your ears and nose do their work and to allow sensations within your body to make themselves felt. Jot down on a piece of paper the things you observe. Try to state your observations accurately and factually: not, "I see a pretty girl in front of me," but, "I see in front of me a mass of long, shiny, black hair falling over the back of a well-fitted red sweater." Let all your nerves work and take in as much as they can.

writing assignment

1. Spend one hour, in one place, writing sentences describing what you are aware of at each moment.
2. Include not only what you see but what you hear, smell, and feel. Include such sensations as the contact of your body with things and the feelings inside your body.
3. Do this as spontaneously as possible. Do not look for something to record, but, as you finish each sentence, record the very first thing you are aware of. Do not worry about repeating yourself. Keep writing steadily. As soon as you finish one sentence, start the next one.
4. Begin each sentence with the words *here and now*.
5. Do not revise. Simply continue writing sentences until the hour is up.

Big Two-Hearted River: Part II

ERNEST HEMINGWAY

In the morning the sun was up and the tent was starting to get hot. Nick crawled out under the mosquito netting stretched across the mouth of the tent, to look at the morning. The grass was wet on his hands as he came out. He held his trousers and his shoes in his hands. The sun was just up over the hill. There was the meadow, the river and the swamp. There were birch trees in the green of the swamp on the other side of the river.

The river was clear and smoothly fast in the early morning. Down about two hundred yards were three logs all the way across the stream. They made the water smooth and deep above them. As Nick watched, a mink crossed the river on the logs and went into the swamp. Nick was excited. He was excited by the early morning and the river. He was really too hurried to eat breakfast, but he knew he must. He built a little fire and put on the coffee pot.

While the water was heating in the pot he took an empty bottle and went down over the edge of the high ground to the meadow. The meadow was wet with dew and Nick wanted to catch grasshoppers for bait before the sun dried the grass. He found plenty of good grasshoppers. They were at the base of the grass stems. Sometimes they clung to a grass stem. They were cold and wet with the dew, and could not jump until the sun warmed them. Nick picked them up, taking only the medium-sized brown ones, and put them into the bottle. He turned over a log and just under the shelter of the edge were several hundred hoppers. It was a grasshopper lodging house. Nick put about fifty of the medium browns into the bottle. While he was picking up the hoppers the others warmed in the sun and commenced to hop away. They flew when they hopped. At first they made one flight and stayed stiff when they landed, as though they were dead.

Nick knew that by the time he was through with breakfast they would be as lively as ever. Without dew in the grass it would take him all day to catch a bottle full of good grasshoppers and he would have to crush many of them, slamming at them with his hat. He washed his hands at the stream. He was excited to be near it. Then he walked up to the tent. The hoppers were already jumping stiffly in the grass. In the bottle, warmed by the sun, they were jumping in a mass. Nick put in a

---

pine stick as a cork. It plugged the mouth of the bottle enough, so the hoppers could not get out and left plenty of air passage.

He had rolled the log back and knew he could get grasshoppers there every morning.

Nick laid the bottle full of jumping grasshoppers against a pine trunk. Rapidly he mixed some buckwheat flour with water and stirred it smooth, one cup of flour, one cup of water. He put a handful of coffee in the pot and dipped a lump of grease out of a can and slid it sputtering across the hot skillet. On the smoking skillet he poured smoothly the buckwheat batter. It spread like lava, the grease spitting sharply. Around the edges the buckwheat cake began to firm, then brown, then crisp. The surface was bubbling slowly to porousness. Nick pushed under the browned under surface with a fresh pine chip. He shook the skillet sideways and the cake was loose on the surface. I won't try and flop it, he thought. He slid the chip of clean wood all the way under the cake, and flopped it over onto its surface. It sputtered in the pan.

When it was cooked Nick regreased the skillet. He used all the batter. It made another big flapjack and one smaller one.

Nick ate a big flapjack and a smaller one, covered with apple butter. He put apple butter on the third cake, folded it over twice, wrapped it in oiled paper and put it in his shirt pocket. He put the apple butter jar back in the pack and cut bread for two sandwiches.

In the pack he found a big onion. He sliced it in two and peeled the silky outer skin. Then he cut one half into slices and made onion sandwiches. He wrapped them in oiled paper and buttoned them in the other pocket of his khaki shirt. He turned the skillet upside down on the grill, drank the coffee, sweetened and yellow brown with condensed milk in it, and tidied up the camp. It was a good camp.

Nick took his fly rod out of the leather rod-case, jointed it, and shoved the rod-case back into the tent. He put on the reel and threaded the line through the guides. He had to hold it from hand to hand, as he threaded it, or it would slip back through its own weight. It was a heavy, double tapered fly line. Nick had paid eight dollars for it a long time ago. It was made heavy to lift back in the air and come forward flat and heavy and straight to make it possible to cast a fly which has no weight. Nick opened the aluminum leader box. The leaders were coiled between the damp flannel pads. Nick had wet the pads at the water cooler on the train up to St. Ignace. In the damp pads the gut leaders had softened and Nick unrolled one and tied it by a loop at the end to the heavy fly line. He fastened a hook on the end of the leader. It was a small hook; very thin and springy.

Nick took it from his hook book, sitting with the rod across his lap. He tested the knot and the spring of the rod by pulling the line taut. It was a good feeling. He was careful not to let the hook bite into his finger.

He started down to the stream, holding his rod, the bottle of grasshoppers hung from his neck by a thong tied in half hitches around the neck of the bottle. His landing net hung by a hook from his belt. Over his shoulder was a long flour sack tied at each corner into an ear. The cord went over his shoulder. The sack flapped against his legs.

Nick felt awkward and professionally happy with all his equipment hanging from him. The grasshopper bottle swung against his chest. In his shirt the breast pockets bulged against him with the lunch and his fly book.

He stepped into the stream. It was a shock. His trousers clung tight to his legs. His shoes felt the gravel. The water was a rising cold shock.

Rushing, the current sucked against his legs. Where he stepped in, the water was over his knees. He waded with the current. The gravel slid under his shoes. He looked down at the swirl of water below each leg and tipped up the bottle to get a grasshopper.

The first grasshopper gave a jump in the neck of the bottle and went out into the water. He was sucked under in a whirl by Nick's right leg and came to the surface a little way down stream. He floated rapidly, kicking. In a quick circle, breaking the smooth surface of the water, he disappeared. A trout had taken him.

Another hopper poked his face out of the bottle. His antennae wavered. He was getting his front legs out of the bottle to jump. Nick took him by the head and held him while he threaded the slim hook under his chin, down through his thorax and into the last segments of his abdomen. The grasshopper took hold of the hook with his feet, spitting tobacco juice on it. Nick dropped him into the water.

Holding the rod in his right hand he let out line against the pull of the grasshopper in the current. He stripped off line from the reel with his left hand and let it run free. He could see the hopper in the little waves of the current. It went out of sight.

There was a tug on the line. Nick pulled against the taut line. It was his first strike. Holding the now living rod across the current, he brought in the line with his left hand. The rod bent in jerks, the trout pumping against the current. Nick knew it was a small one. He lifted the rod straight up in the air. It bowed with the pull.

He saw the trout in the water jerking with his head and body against the shifting tangent of the line in the stream.

Nick took the line in his left hand and pulled the trout, thumping tiredly against the current, to the surface. His back was mottled the clear, water-over-gravel color, his side flashing in the sun. The rod under his right arm, Nick stooped, dipping his right hand into the current. He held the trout, never still, with his moist right hand, while he unhooked the barb from his mouth, then dropped him back into the stream.

He hung unsteadily in the current, then settled to the bottom beside a stone. Nick reached down his hand to touch him, his arm to the elbow under water. The trout was steady in the moving stream, resting on the gravel, beside a stone. As Nick's fingers touched him, touched his smooth, cool, underwater feeling he was gone, gone in a shadow across the bottom of the stream.

He's all right, Nick thought. He was only tired.

He had wet his hand before he touched the trout, so he would not disturb the delicate mucus that covered him. If a trout was touched with a dry hand, a white fungus attacked the unprotected spot. Years before when he had fished crowded streams, with fly fishermen ahead of him and behind him, Nick had again and again come on dead trout, furry with white fungus, drifted against a rock, or floating belly up in some pool. Nick did not like to fish with other men on the river. Unless they were of your party, they spoiled it.

He wallowed down the stream, above his knees in the current, through the fifty yards of shallow water above the pile of logs that crossed the stream. He did not rebait his hook and held it in his hand as he waded. He was certain he could catch small trout in the shallows, but he did not want them. There would be no big trout in the shallows this time of day.

Now the water deepened up his thighs sharply and coldly. Ahead was the smooth dammed-back flood of water above the logs. The water was smooth and dark; on the left, the lower edge of the meadow; on the right the swamp.

Nick leaned back against the current and took a hopper from the bottle. He threaded the hopper on the hook and spat on him for good luck. Then he pulled several yards of line from the reel and tossed the hopper out ahead onto the fast, dark water. It floated down towards the logs, then the weight of the line pulled the bait under the surface. Nick held the rod in his right hand, letting the line run out through his fingers.

There was a long tug. Nick struck and the rod came alive and dangerous, bent double, the line tightening, coming out of water, tightening, all in a heavy, dangerous, steady pull. Nick felt the moment when the leader would break if the strain increased and let the line go.

The reel ratcheted into a mechanical shriek as the line went out in a rush. Too fast. Nick could not check it, the line rushing out, the reel note rising as the line ran out.

With the core of the reel showing, his heart feeling stopped with the excitement, leaning back against the current that mounted icily his thighs, Nick thumbed the reel hard with his left hand. It was awkward getting his thumb inside the fly reel frame.

As he put on pressure the line tightened into sudden hardness and beyond the logs a huge trout went high out of water. As he jumped, Nick lowered the tip of the rod. But he felt, as he dropped the tip to ease the strain, the moment when the strain was too great; the hardness too tight. Of course, the leader had broken. There was no mistaking the feeling when all spring left the line and it became dry and hard. Then it went slack.

His mouth dry, his heart down, Nick reeled in. He had never seen so big a trout. There was a heaviness, a power not to be held, and then the bulk of him, as he jumped. He looked as broad as a salmon.

Nick's hand was shaky. He reeled in slowly. The thrill had been too much. He felt, vaguely, a little sick, as though it would be better to sit down.

The leader had broken where the hook was tied to it. Nick took it in his hand. He thought of the trout somewhere on the bottom, holding himself steady over the gravel, far down below the light, under the logs, with the hook in his jaw. Nick knew the trout's teeth would cut through the snell of the hook. The hook would imbed itself in his jaw. He'd bet the trout was angry. Anything that size would be angry. That was a trout. He had been solidly hooked. Solid as a rock. He felt like a rock, too, before he started off. By God, he was a big one. By God, he was the biggest one I ever heard of.

Nick climbed out onto the meadow and stood, water running down his trousers and out of his shoes, his shoes squelchy. He went over and sat on the logs. He did not want to rush his sensations any.

He wriggled his toes in the water, in his shoes, and got out a cigarette from his breast pocket. He lit it and tossed the match into the fast water below the logs. A tiny trout rose at the match, as it swung around in the fast current. Nick laughed. He would finish the cigarette.

He sat on the logs, smoking, drying in the sun, the sun warm on his back, the river shallow ahead entering the woods, curving into the woods, shallows, light glittering, big water-smooth rocks, cedars along the bank and white birches, the logs warm in the sun, smooth to sit on, without bark, gray to the touch; slowly the feeling of disappointment left him. It went away slowly, the feeling of disappointment that came sharply after the thrill that made his shoulders ache. It was all right now. His rod lying out on the logs, Nick tied a new hook on the leader, pulling the gut tight until it grimped into itself in a hard knot.

He baited up, then picked up the rod and walked to the far end of the logs to get into the water, where it was not too deep. Under and beyond the logs was a deep pool. Nick walked around the shallow shelf near the swamp shore until he came out on the shallow bed of the stream.

On the left, where the meadow ended and the woods began, a great elm tree was uprooted. Gone over in a storm, it lay back into the woods, its roots clotted with dirt, grass growing in them, rising a solid bank beside the stream. The river cut to the edge of the uprooted tree. From where Nick stood he could see deep channels, like ruts, cut in the shallow bed of the stream by the flow of the current. Pebbly where he stood and pebbly and full of boulders beyond; where it curved near the tree roots, the bed of the stream was marly and between the ruts of deep water green weed fronds swung in the current.

Nick swung the rod back over his shoulder and forward, and the line, curving forward, laid the grasshopper down on one of the deep channels in the weeds. A trout struck and Nick hooked him.

Holding the rod far out toward the uprooted tree and sloshing backward in the current, Nick worked the trout, plunging, the rod bending alive, out of the danger of the weeds into the open river. Holding the rod, pumping alive against the current, Nick brought the trout in. He rushed, but always came, the spring of the rod yielding to the rushes, sometimes jerking under the water, but always bringing him in. Nick eased downstream with the rushes. The rod above his head he led the trout over the net, then lifted.

The trout hung heavy in the net, mottled trout back and silver sides in the meshes. Nick unhooked him; heavy sides, good to hold, big undershot jaw, and slipped him, heaving and big sliding, into the long sack that hung from his shoulders in the water.

Nick spread the mouth of the sack against the current and it filled, heavy with water. He held it up, the bottom in the stream, and the water poured out through the sides. Inside at the bottom was the big trout, alive in the water.

Nick moved downstream. The sack out ahead of him sunk heavy in the water, pulling from his shoulders.

It was getting hot, the sun hot on the back of his neck.

Nick had one good trout. He did not care about getting many trout. Now the stream was shallow and wide. There were trees along both banks. The trees of the left bank made short shadows on the current in the forenoon sun. Nick knew there were trout in each shadow. In the afternoon, after the sun had crossed toward the hills, the trout would be in the cool shadows on the other side of the stream.

The very biggest ones would lie up close to the bank. You could always pick them up there on the Black. When the sun was down they all moved out into the current. Just when the sun made the water blinding in the glare before it went down, you were liable to strike a big trout anywhere in the current. It was almost impossible to fish then, the surface of the water was blinding as a mirror in the sun. Of course, you could fish upstream, but in a stream like the Black, or this, you had to wallow against the current and in a deep place, the water piled up on you. It was no fun to fish upstream with this much current.

Nick moved along through the shallow stretch watching the banks for deep holes. A beech tree grew close beside the river, so that the branches hung down into the water. The stream went back in under the leaves. There were always trout in a place like that.

Nick did not care about fishing that hole. He was sure he would get hooked in the branches.

It looked deep though. He dropped the grasshopper so the current took it under water, back in under the overhanging branch. The line pulled hard and Nick struck. The trout threshed heavily, half out of water in the leaves and branches. The line was caught. Nick pulled hard and the trout was off. He reeled in and holding the hook in his hand, walked down the stream.

Ahead, close to the left bank, was a big log. Nick saw it was hollow; pointing up river the current entered it smoothly, only a little ripple spread each side of the log. The water was deepening. The top of the hollow log was gray and dry. It was partly in the shadow.

Nick took the cork out of the grasshopper bottle and a hopper clung to it. He picked him off, hooked him and tossed him out. He held the rod far out so that the hopper on the water moved into the current flowing into the hollow log. Nick lowered the rod and the hopper floated in. There was a heavy strike. Nick swung the rod against the pull. It felt as though he were hooked into the log itself, except for the live feeling.

He tried to force the fish out into the current. It came, heavily.

The line went slack and Nick thought the trout was gone. Then he saw him, very near, in the current, shaking his head, trying to get the hook out. His mouth was clamped shut. He was fighting the hook in the clear flowing current.

Looping in the line with his left hand, Nick swung the rod to make the line taut and tried to lead the trout toward the net, but he was gone, out of sight, the line pumping. Nick fought him against the current, letting him thump in the water against the spring of the rod. He shifted the rod to his left hand, worked the trout upstream, holding his weight, fighting on the rod, and then let him down into the net. He lifted him clear of the water, a heavy half circle in the net, the net dripping, unhooked him and slid him into the sack.

He spread the mouth of the sack and looked down in at the two big trout alive in the water.

Through the deepening water, Nick waded over to the hollow log. He took the sack off, over his head, the trout flopping as it came out of water, and hung it so the trout were deep in the water. Then he pulled himself up on the log and sat, the water from his trousers and boots running down into the stream. He laid his rod down, moved along to the shady end of the log and took the sandwiches out of his pocket. He dipped the sandwiches in the cold water. The current carried away the crumbs. He ate the sandwiches and dipped his hat full of water to drink, the water running out through his hat just ahead of his drinking.

It was cool in the shade, sitting on the log. He took a cigarette out and struck a match to light it. The match sunk into the gray wood, making a tiny furrow. Nick leaned over the side of the log, found a hard place and lit the match. He sat smoking and watching the river.

Ahead the river narrowed and went into a swamp. The river became smooth and deep and the swamp looked solid with cedar trees, their trunks close together, their branches solid. It would not be possible to walk through a swamp like that. The branches grew so low. You would have to keep almost level with the ground to move at all. You could not crash through the branches. That must be why the animals that lived in swamps were built the way they were, Nick thought.

He wished he had brought something to read. He felt like reading. He did not feel like going on into the swamp. He looked down the river. A big cedar slanted all the way across the stream. Beyond that the river went into the swamp.

Nick did not want to go in there now. He felt a reaction against deep wading with the water deepening up under his armpits, to hook big trout in places impossible to land them. In the swamp the banks were bare, the big cedars came together overhead, the sun did not come through, except in patches; in the fast deep water, in the half light, the fishing would be tragic. In the swamp fishing was a tragic adventure. Nick did not want it. He did not want to go down the stream any further today.

He took out his knife, opened it and stuck it in the log. Then he pulled up the sack, reached into it and brought out one of the trout. Holding him near the tail, hard to hold, alive, in his hand, he whacked him against the log. The trout quivered, rigid. Nick laid him on the log in the shade and broke the neck of the other fish the same way. He laid them side by side on the log. They were fine trout.

Nick cleaned them, slitting them from the vent to the tip of the jaw. All the insides and the gills and tongue came out in one piece. They were both males; long gray-white strips of milt, smooth and clean. All the insides clean and compact, coming out all together. Nick tossed the offal ashore for the minks to find.

He washed the trout in the stream. When he held them back up in the water they looked like live fish. Their color was not gone yet. He washed his hands and dried them on the log. Then he laid the trout on the sack spread out on the log, rolled them up in it, tied the bundle and put it in the landing net. His knife was still standing, blade stuck in the log. He cleaned it on the wood and put it in his pocket.

Nick stood up on the log, holding his rod, the landing net hanging heavy, then stepped into the water and splashed ashore. He climbed the bank and cut up into the woods, toward the high ground. He was going back to camp. He looked back. The river just showed through the trees. There were plenty of days coming when he could fish the swamp.

---

1. Hemingway uses all the senses to make Nick's experience vivid to the reader. Where do you find the sense of *hearing* used?
2. Pick out passages in which he tries to communicate the sense of *bodily movement* or the sense of the force, weight, or balance of things the body is in contact with. (This is called the *kinesthetic* sense.)
3. Where do you find the sense of *touch* – the feel of things against the skin?
4. Are any *smells* recorded or suggested?
5. What senses do you find Hemingway most aware of? Least aware of?
6. Do you feel that there are parts of the environment with which Hemingway is not in contact? What are they?

class writing exercise

Sit for a minute or two, turning on all your senses. What feeling do your surroundings give you? Make a *generalization* about the classroom that reflects your strongest feeling about it and write this generalization down as a sentence. For example, let us say the multitude of sights and sounds and movements and smells in the room gives you a feeling of confusion; then you would write a sentence like this: "I am confused by the many things going on around me in my English classroom."

Now develop this idea into a *paragraph*. A paragraph is simply a collection of *specifics,* in the form of sentences, built around one generalization and indicated by a single indention, about five letters wide, at the beginning. You have already written your generalization. Put it at the top of your paragraph, indented. Then, without indenting again, fill the paragraph with specific sentences describing the different things going on around you, sentences like "I am aware of hands with pens in them moving all around me, and I can hear the scratching of the pens on paper."

Do not use any further generalizations. Just fill up your paragraph with examples, making sure that each example illustrates the feeling you expressed in your original generalization. This generalization, around which you are building your paragraph, is called a *topic sentence*.

sketching assignment

Like the first sketching assignment, this one may be done either outdoors or in the classroom. This time, instead of picking out an object to sketch, try to give a quick, lively impression of your whole surroundings. Again, *work from large to small,* putting in the large, obvious things first and working down to the smaller things. Use all your senses: include sounds, smells, feelings of motion, and temperature – everything you can take in.

The Great Figure

WILLIAM CARLOS WILLIAMS

Among the rain
and lights
I saw the figure 5
in gold
on a red
firetruck
moving
tense
unheeded
to gong clangs
siren howls
and wheels rumbling
through the dark city.

---

1. Wallace Stevens in "A Study of Two Pears" focuses our attention on the objects, emphasizing their stillness and stability. Williams' poem, on the other hand, is full of movement. While Stevens' poem is like a photograph of its subject, Williams' poem, like a television camera, follows the figure 5 on the firetruck in such a way that it is the only still thing in a rush of noise and movement. What are some of the things that move in the poem?
2. Why do you think Williams chooses a number, rather than, say, a headlight or a ladder to focus upon? What is stable and still about a number?
3. Besides a number, can you think of any other things that are always and everywhere the same ?
4. A number is a device for making order out of the chaos of our experience. What are some other ways of ordering experience? Do you use any of them yourself?
5. Does Nick, in "Big Two-Hearted River," do anything to make order out of the chaos of experience?

---

1. The title of Demuth's painting indicates, of course, that he was inspired to paint it by William Carlos Williams' "The Great Figure." What other obvious clues did he include that point to the poem?
2. Willem Kalf, in his *Still Life,* shows objects in repose, much as Stevens shows us the two pears. Demuth, on the other hand, shows us *movement*. What are some of the devices he uses to give us the feeling of movement?
3. Take each line in Williams' poem and see if you can find evidence that Demuth tries to put the idea of that line into his picture. For example, how does he convey the feeling in the word "tense"? What does he fail to get across? What does he communicate best?

PLATE II

I SAW THE FIGURE 5 IN GOLD: Charles Demuth The Metropolitan Museum of Art, The Alfred Stieglitz Collection, 1949

3

perceiving emotional attitudes

Lack of sensitivity is perhaps basically an unawareness of ourselves.

—*Eric Hoffer*

You are not separate from your environment. This may seem, at first, an odd statement. But think about it.

Physically, the elements of your body are constantly changing, being discarded and renewed. It is said that even your bones replace themselves every few years. Literally, you are what you eat and breathe – parts of your environment.

It is impossible to think of something that does not stem from observations of your environment. Try it. Even a little green Mars man in your imagination is made up of qualities that you have observed, such as the color green. Try to imagine a nonexistent color!

Psychologically, you observe everything in the way you have learned to observe it from teaching or from earlier examples. Imagine a prehistoric man coming upon a new Chevrolet. He would not see metal, paint, glass, wheels, rubber; he does not know what any of these things are. He would see a frightening shape, entirely meaningless to him.

You see in things patterns and emotions that are already inside you. In a sense, you *are* your environment.

Some of these attitudes, results of good advice or your own experience, are sensible. An attitude of avoidance in the presence of a coiled rattlesnake, for example, is healthy.

However, some of these attitudes result from poor advice or insufficient experience. A person who has handled snakes and learned about them is not afraid of them; he knows how to approach them, and he knows that many of them are clean, harmless, and even beneficial. You are likely to trust what is familiar to you and distrust what is unfamiliar.

Many attitudes are not really your own at all, but are prejudices forced upon you by the people around you. A person who has never seen a snake may fear snakes because his parents or associates have "indoctrinated" him with an unreasonable attitude. Children are exposed to prejudices toward racial, social, and national groups before they have the chance to become acquainted with particular members of these groups; they adopt such prejudices in order to avoid conflict with their own group, and eventually they may come to believe that the attitudes are their own. Later, if they find themselves members of a larger and more enlightened group, a conflict arises between what they see before their eyes and what they have been "taught" to believe. In D. H. Lawrence's poem, "Snake," the author discovers a conflict between his real feelings and the attitude which he has been taught.

In this writing assignment and some of the later ones you will begin to explore your attitudes toward things and people – those attitudes that make you see them the way you do.

writing assignment

1. Spend one hour, in one place, writing sentences describing what you are aware of at each moment. You may use the same place you did for the writing assignment in Unit 2, or you may wish to try a new place.
2. Again, use all your senses. But this time try to examine and record your emotional attitude, however slight, toward each sensation. If a sound is faintly annoying, if a smell reminds you of something, or if an object your eye lights upon calls up an association or is pleasing in some way, try to find words to express the feeling you have about it. Try to trace the *origin* of the feeling. What experience or teaching can you associate with it? Let us say, for instance, you find that you dislike something white; do you associate it with a hospital? If the sound of a lawnmower annoys you, is it because you had to mow the lawn when you didn't want to? Or is it because someone in your family is always complaining about the noise lawnmowers make? Ask yourself, why?
3. Begin each sentence with the words *here and now*.
4. Again, do not revise or worry about correctness. Just get one idea down and go on to the next.

class writing exercise

Look over your sentences from the writing assignment. See if you can come to some conclusion — a generalization — about what sorts of sense impressions please you. Write this generalization down in the form of a *topic sentence,* something like, "I enjoy sights, sounds, and smells that remind me of the comforts of home," for example. Then develop a paragraph of sentences, each one of which describes a sensation and tells what pleasant experience you associate with it.

Arrangement in Black and White

DOROTHY PARKER

The woman with the pink velvet poppies twined round the assisted gold of her hair traversed the crowded room at an interesting gait combining a skip with a sidle, and clutched the lean arm of her host.

"Now I got you!" she said. "Now you can't get away!"

"Why, hello," said her host. "Well. How are you?"

"Oh, I'm finely," she said. "Just simply finely. Listen. I want you to do me the most terrible favor. Will you? Will you please? Pretty please?"

"What is it?" said her host.

"Listen," she said. "I want to meet Walter Williams. Honestly, I'm just simply crazy about that man. Oh, when he sings! When he sings those spirituals! Well, I said to Burton, 'It's a good thing for you Walter Williams is colored,' I said, 'or you'd have lots of reason to be jealous.' I'd really love to meet him. I'd like to tell him I've heard him sing. Will you be an angel and introduce me to him?"

"Why, certainly," said her host. "I thought you'd met him. The party's for him. Where is he, anyway?"

"He's over there by the bookcase," she said. "Let's wait till those people get through talking to him. Well, I think you're simply marvelous, giving this perfectly marvelous party for him, and having him meet all these white people, and all. Isn't he terribly grateful?"

"I hope not," said her host.

"I think it's really terribly nice," she said. "I do. I don't see why on earth it isn't perfectly all right to meet colored people. I haven't any feeling at all about it — not one single bit. Burton — oh, he's just the other way. Well, you know, he comes from Virginia, and you know how they are."

"Did he come tonight?" said her host.

"No, he couldn't," she said. "I'm a regular grass widow tonight. I told him when I left, 'There's no telling what I'll do,' I said. He was just so tired out, he couldn't move. Isn't it a shame?"

"Ah," said her host.

"Wait till I tell him I met Walter Williams!" she said. "He'll just about die. Oh, we have more arguments about colored people. I talk to him like I don't know what, I get so excited. 'Oh, don't be so silly,' I say. But I must say for Burton, he's heaps broader-minded than lots of these Southerners. He's really awfully fond of colored people. Well, he says himself, he wouldn't have white servants. And you know, he had this old colored nurse, this regular old nigger mammy, and he just simply loves her. Why, every time he goes home, he goes out in the kitchen to see her. He does, really, to this day. All he says is, he says he hasn't got a word to say against colored people as long as they keep their place. He's always doing things for them — giving them clothes and I don't know what all. The only thing he says, he says he wouldn't sit down at the table with one for a million dollars. 'Oh,' I say to him, 'you make me sick, talking like that.' I'm just terrible to him. Aren't I terrible?"

"Oh, no, no, no," said her host. "No, no."

"I am," she said. "I know I am. Poor Burton! Now, me, I don't feel that way at all. I haven't the slightest feeling about colored people. Why, I'm just crazy about some of them. They're just like children — just as easygoing, and always singing and laughing and everything. Aren't they the happiest things you ever saw in your life? Honestly, it makes me laugh just to hear them. Oh, I like them. I really do. Well, now, listen, I have this colored laundress, I've had her for years, and I'm devoted to her. She's a real character. And I want to tell you, I think of her as my friend. That's the way I think of her. As I say to Burton, 'Well, for Heaven's sakes, we're all human beings!' Aren't we?"

"Yes," said her host. "Yes, indeed."

"Now this Walter Williams," she said. "I think a man like that's a real artist. I do. I think he deserves an awful lot of credit. Goodness, I'm so crazy about music or anything, I don't care *what* color he is. I honestly think if a person's an artist, nobody ought to have any feeling at all about meeting them. That's absolutely what I say to Burton. Don't you think I'm right?"

"Yes," said her host. "Oh, yes."

"That's the way I feel," she said. "I just can't understand people being narrow-minded. Why, I absolutely think it's a privilege to meet a man like Walter Williams. Yes, I do. I haven't any feeling at all. Well, my goodness, the good Lord made him, just the same as He did any of us. Didn't He?"

"Surely," said her host. "Yes, indeed."

"That's what I say," she said. "Oh, I get so furious when people are narrow-minded about colored people. It's just all I can do not to say something. Of course, I do admit when you get a bad colored man, they're simply terrible. But as I say to Burton, there are some bad white people, too, in this world. Aren't there?"

"I guess there are," said her host.

"Why, I'd really be glad to have a man like Walter Williams come to my house and sing for us, some time," she said. "Of course, I couldn't ask him on account of Burton, but I wouldn't have any feeling about it at all. Oh, can't he sing! Isn't it marvelous, the way they all have music in them? It just seems to be right *in* them. Come on, let's go on over and talk to him. Listen, what shall I do when I'm introduced? Ought I to shake hands? Or what?"

"Why, do whatever you want," said her host.

"I guess maybe I'd better," she said. "I wouldn't for the world have him think I had any feeling. I think I'd better shake hands, just the way I would with anybody else. That's just exactly what I'll do."

They reached the tall young Negro, standing by the bookcase. The host performed introductions; the Negro bowed.

"How do you do?" he said.

The woman with the pink velvet poppies extended her hand at the length of her arm and held it so for all the world to see, until the Negro took it, shook it, and gave it back to her.

"Oh, how do you do, Mr. Williams," she said. "Well, how do you do. I've just been saying, I've enjoyed your singing so awfully much. I've been to your concerts, and we have you on the phonograph and everything. Oh, I just enjoy it!"

She spoke with great distinctness, moving her lips meticulously, as if in parlance with the deaf.

"I'm so glad," he said.

"I'm just simply crazy about that 'Water Boy' thing you sing," she said. "Honestly, I can't get it out of my head. I have my husband nearly crazy, the way I go around humming it all the time. Oh, he looks just as black as the ace of – Well. Tell me, where on earth do you ever get all those songs of yours? How do you ever get hold of them?"

"Why," he said, "there are so many different –"

"I should think you'd love singing them," she said. "It must be more fun. All those darling old spirituals – oh, I just love them! Well, what are you doing, now? Are you still keeping up your singing? Why don't you have another concert, some time?"

"I'm having one the sixteenth of this month," he said.

"Well, I'll be there," she said. "I'll be there, if I possibly can. You can count on me. Goodness, here comes a whole raft of people to talk to you. You're just a regular guest of honor! Oh, who's that girl in white? I've seen her some place."

"That's Katherine Burke," said her host.

"Good Heavens," she said, "is that Katherine Burke? Why, she looks entirely different off the stage. I thought she was much better-looking. I had no idea she was so terribly dark. Why, she looks almost like – Oh, I think she's a wonderful actress! Don't you think she's a wonderful actress, Mr. Williams? Oh, I think she's marvelous. Don't you?"

"Yes, I do," he said.

"Oh, I do, too," she said. "Just wonderful. Well, goodness, we must give someone else a chance to talk to the guest of honor. Now, don't forget, Mr. Williams, I'm going to be at that concert if I possibly can. I'll be there applauding like everything. And if I can't come, I'm going to tell everybody I know to go, anyway. Don't you forget!"

"I won't," he said, "Thank you so much."

The host took her arm and piloted her into the next room.

"Oh, my dear," she said. "I nearly died! Honestly, I give you my word, I nearly passed away. Did you hear that terrible break I made? I was just going to say Katherine Burke looked almost like a nigger. I just caught myself in time. Oh, do you think he noticed?"

"I don't believe so," said her host.

"Well, thank goodness," she said, "because I wouldn't have embarrassed him for anything. Why, he's awfully nice. Just as nice as he can be. Nice manners, and everything. You know, so many colored people, you give them an inch, and they walk all over you. But he doesn't try any of that. Well, he's got more sense, I suppose. He's really nice. Don't you think so?"

"Yes," said her host.

"I liked him," she said. "I haven't any feeling at all because he's a colored man. I felt just as natural as I would with anybody. Talked to him as naturally, and everything. But honestly, I could hardly keep a straight face. I kept thinking of Burton. Oh, wait till I tell Burton I called him 'Mister'!"

1. The "heroine" of this little episode insists repeatedly that she has no racial prejudice. What are some specific speeches and actions that show she is wrong?
2. What are some evidences that she "stereotypes" Negroes — that is, thinks of them as "all alike" instead of as individuals?
3. Where do you think her attitudes come from? In what kind of group would they be accepted? How does she appear to the group she is in here?
4. Can you find evidence that the author of the story "stereotypes" any of her characters?
5. Can you think of any occasions in the past in which you have betrayed prejudices which you had been taught, but which were not accepted by the group you were in?
6. Make a generalization in answer to the following question: What parts of her environment is this woman not in contact with?

Snake

D. H. LAWRENCE

A snake came to my water-trough
On a hot, hot day, and I in pyjamas for the heat,
To drink there.

In the deep, strange-scented shade of the great dark carob-tree
I came down the steps with my pitcher
And must wait, must stand and wait, for there he was at the trough before me.
He reached down from a fissure in the earth-wall in the gloom
And trailed his yellow-brown slackness soft-bellied down, over the edge of the
stone trough
And rested his throat upon the stone bottom,
And where the water had dripped from the tap, in a small clearness,
He sipped with his straight mouth,

Softly drank through his straight gums, into his slack long body,
Silently.

Someone was before me at my water-trough,
And I, like a second comer, waiting.

He lifted his head from his drinking, as cattle do,
And looked at me vaguely, as drinking cattle do,
And flickered his two-forked tongue from his lips, and mused a moment,
And stooped and drank a little more,
Being earth brown, earth golden from the burning bowels of the earth
On the day of Sicilian July, with Etna smoking.

The voice of my education said to me
He must be killed,
For in Sicily the black, black snakes are innocent, the gold are venomous.

And voices in me said, If you were a man
You would take a stick and break him now, and finish him off.

But I must confess how I liked him,
How glad I was he had come like a guest in quiet, to drink at my water-trough
And depart peaceful, pacified, and thankless,
Into the burning bowels of this earth.

Was it cowardice, that I dared not kill him?
Was it perversity, that I longed to talk to him?
Was it humility, to feel so honoured?
I felt so honoured.

And yet those voices:
If you were not afraid, you would kill him!

And truly I was afraid, I was most afraid,
But even so, honoured still more
That he should seek my hospitality
From out the dark door of the secret earth.

He drank enough
And lifted his head, dreamily, as one who has drunken,
And flickered his tongue like a forked night on the air, so black,
Seeming to lick his lips,
And looked around like a god, unseeing, into the air,
And slowly turned his head,
And slowly, very slowly, as if thrice adream,

Proceeded to draw his slow length curving round
And climb again the broken bank of my wall-face.

And as he put his head into that dreadful hole,
And as he slowly drew up, snake-easing his shoulders, and entered farther,
A sort of horror, a sort of protest against his withdrawing into that horrid black
 hole,
Deliberately going into the blackness, and slowly drawing himself after,
Overcame me now his back was turned.
I looked round, I put down my pitcher
I picked up a clumsy log
And threw it at the water-trough with a clatter.

I think it did not hit him.
But suddenly that part of him that was left behind convulsed in undignified haste,
Writhed like lightning, and was gone
Into the black hole, the earth-lipped fissure in the wallfront,
At which, in the intense still noon, I stared with fascination.

And immediately I regretted it.
I thought how paltry, how vulgar, what a mean act!
I despised myself and the voices of my accursed human education.

And I thought of the albatross,*
And I wished he would come back, my snake.

For he seemed to me again like a king,
Like a king in exile, uncrowned in the underworld,
Now due to be crowned again.

And so, I missed my chance with one of the lords
Of life.
And I have something to expiate;
A pettiness.

---

* In Coleridge's *Rime of the Ancient Mariner,* the narrator, a sailor, kills an albatross, a bird of good omen. Its body is hung around the sailor's neck as a constant reminder of his crime. Thus the albatross has become a symbol of penance and the burden of guilt.

1. What reasons are there for killing the snake? What reasons are there for *not* killing it ?
2. Does Lawrence fail to kill the snake because he is afraid of it? What are his natural feelings toward it?
3. Exactly what makes him feel shame (as he expresses it in the last four stanzas)? What does he mean by the "voices of my accursed human education"? Could he have had any other kind of education?
4. A fear of snakes, even harmless snakes, is common in our culture. What might be some of the origins of that fear? Does Lawrence hint at any of them in the poem?
5. What *senses* does Lawrence use to convey his feeling about the snake?
6. In the description of the match in Unit 1, analogy is used to help give a clear picture. Does Lawrence use analogy to help us perceive the snake clearly? Where?
7. Do you feel that Lawrence's contact with his environment is good or poor? Explain your answer in terms of emotional attitudes.

---

1. What is your immediate reaction to this painting?
2. What are the chief ingredients of the painting? Would you place any value on them if you possessed them? Why not?
3. What associations or teachings have created this emotional attitude toward the objects?
4. Imagine, again, the primitive man coming upon the new Chevrolet. Would he value it? Why not? What are his values likely to be based upon ?
5. You probably keep a good many "useless" objects around because they are "attractive" — things like vases (and the flowers that go in them), pictures, and other "decorations." How, exactly, are they more attractive than the objects in this painting? What standard do you use?
6. When you were a child, would you have enjoyed these objects? (See the quotation from Mary Wortley Montague at the beginning of Unit 1.)
7. Does this picture suggest to you any sense impressions other than those of sight? Which ones? What parts of the picture suggest them?
8. Do you think that a painting like this might help you make contact with your environment? In what ways?

PLATE III

RESERVOIR: Robert Rauschenberg From *Art: U.S.A.,* the Johnson Collection

Drawing by Al Ross in the *Saturday Review*

4

perceiving thoughts

Habit: a shackle for the free.
—*Ambrose Bierce*

Your mind is made up of impressions from your senses and of connections among these impressions. It is at the same time part of your "self" and part of your environment. The connections that it makes are what we call "thoughts," and these thoughts, or patterns of relationship among impressions, are often reinforced by association with emotions.

Sometimes these emotionally strengthened thoughts are original and valuable: they may be the source of invention and creativity, or they may be marks of desirable individuality. A Jefferson, an Einstein, or a Picasso is a man whose mind runs persistently in paths little frequented by others, a man who finds truths not discovered by others.

On the other hand, these thoughts may become unvarying patterns or emotionally charged images which repeat themselves over and over, a little like the familiar broken record. They are then what we call *obsessions*. These minor obsessions are normal; we all have them. Sex, clothes, and cars are common ones. Others may be social or financial: these are the ones we call "worries." Whatever they are about, whether pleasant or unpleasant, these repetitious thoughts can interfere with concentration, intruding at the most inconvenient times, as when we are trying to study. They form a kind of background static which frequently drowns out our more constructive mental activities.

The following assignment may help you to identify and evaluate some of these random thoughts in your own mind.

writing assignment

1. As in the previous two assignments, find a place where you can sit undisturbed for an hour. Again, write sentences beginning *here and now*.
2. From time to time you will probably find your mind drifting off; you may stop observing and writing, and start "thinking" about something which has wandered into your mind.
3. Each time this happens, try to catch and identify the idea or image which *first* appeared in your mind to distract you. Write down what it was; then quickly evaluate it. Was it a useful or pleasurable thought, or was it an often-repeated, broken-record worry or fantasy? When you have made this quick evaluation, go on immediately to record sensations until another thought intrudes. Try to "ambush" as many involuntary thoughts as you can this way.
4. Above all, be spontaneous. Don't censor. Don't think about what you are "supposed to" think, or what will "look good."
5. When you have finished your hour, look over what you have written down, and see if you can add a sentence summing up what sorts of things seem to come into your mind.

class writing exercise

Make a generalization about what kinds of thoughts seem to wander into your mind when you are trying to concentrate. Construct a paragraph of specific examples around this topic sentence.

The Second Tree from the Corner

E. B. WHITE

"Ever had any bizarre thoughts?" asked the doctor.

Mr. Trexler failed to catch the word. "What kind?" he said.

"Bizarre," repeated the doctor, his voice steady. He watched his patient for any slight change of expression, any wince. It seemed to Trexler that the doctor was not only watching him closely but was creeping slowly toward him, like a lizard toward a bug. Trexler shoved his chair back an inch and gathered himself for a reply. He was about to say "Yes" when he realized that if he said yes the next question would be unanswerable. Bizarre thoughts, bizarre thoughts? Ever have any bizarre thoughts? What kind of thoughts *except* bizarre had he had since the age of two?

Trexler felt the time passing, the necessity for an answer. These psychiatrists were busy men, overloaded, not to be kept waiting. The next patient was probably already perched out there in the waiting room, lonely, worried, shifting around on the sofa, his mind stuffed with bizarre thoughts and amorphous fears. Poor bastard, thought Trexler. Out there all alone in that misshapen antechamber, staring at the filing cabinet and wondering whether to tell the doctor about that day on the Madison Avenue bus.

Let's see, bizarre thoughts. Trexler dodged back along the dreadful corridor of the years to see what he could find. He felt the doctor's eyes upon him and knew that time was running out. Don't be so conscientious, he said to himself. If a bizarre thought is indicated here, just reach into the bag and pick anything at all. A man as well supplied with bizarre thoughts as you are should have no difficulty producing one for the record. Trexler darted into the bag, hung for a moment before one of his thoughts, as a hummingbird pauses in the delphinium. No, he said, not that one. He darted to another (the one about the rhesus monkey), paused, considered. No, he said, not that.

Trexler knew he must hurry. He had already used up pretty nearly four seconds since the question had been put. But it was an impossible situation – just one more lousy, impossible situation such as he was always getting himself into. When, he asked himself, are you going to quit maneuvering yourself into a pocket? He made one more effort. This time

---

he stopped at the asylum, only the bars were lucite – fluted, retractable. Not here, he said. Not this one.

He looked straight at the doctor. "No," he said quietly. "I never have any bizarre thoughts."

The doctor sucked in on his pipe, blew a plume of smoke toward the rows of medical books. Trexler's gaze followed the smoke. He managed to make out one of the titles, "The Genito-Urinary System." A bright wave of fear swept cleanly over him, and he winced under the first pain of kidney stones. He remembered when he was a child, the first time he ever entered a doctor's office, sneaking a look at the titles of the books – and the flush of fear, the shirt wet under his arms, the book on t.b., the sudden knowledge that he was in the advanced stages of consumption, the quick vision of the hemorrhage. Trexler sighed wearily. Forty years, he thought, and I still get thrown by the title of a medical book. Forty years and I still can't stay on life's little bucky horse. No wonder I'm sitting here in this dreary joint at the end of this woebegone afternoon, lying about my bizarre thoughts to a doctor who looks, come to think of it, rather tired.

The session dragged on. After about twenty minutes, the doctor rose and knocked his pipe out. Trexler got up, knocked the ashes out of his brain, and waited. The doctor smiled warmly and stuck out his hand. "There's nothing the matter with you – you're just scared. Want to know how I know you're scared?"

"How?" asked Trexler.

"Look at the chair you've been sitting in! See how it has moved back away from my desk? You kept inching away from me while I asked you questions. That means you're scared."

"Does it?" said Trexler, faking a grin. "Yeah, I suppose it does."

They finished shaking hands. Trexler turned and walked out uncertainly along the passage, then into the waiting room and out past the next patient, a ruddy pin-striped man who was seated on the sofa twirling his hat nervously and staring straight ahead at the files. Poor, frightened guy, thought Trexler, he's probably read in the *Times* that one American male out of every two is going to die of heart disease by twelve o'clock next Thursday. It says that in the paper almost every morning. And he's also probably thinking about that day on the Madison Avenue bus.

A week later, Trexler was back in the patient's chair. And for several weeks thereafter he continued to visit the doctor, always toward the end of the afternoon, when the vapors hung thick above the pool of the mind and darkened the whole region of the East Seventies. He felt no better as time went on, and he found it impossible to work. He discovered that the visits were becoming routine and that although the routine was one to which he certainly did not look forward, at least he could accept it with cool resignation, as once, years ago, he had accepted a long spell with a dentist who had settled down to a steady fooling with a couple of dead teeth. The visits, moreover, were now assuming a pattern recognizable to the patient.

Each session would begin with a résumé of symptoms — the dizziness in the streets, the constricting pain in the back of the neck, the apprehensions, the tightness of the scalp, the inability to concentrate, the despondency and the melancholy times, the feeling of pressure and tension, the anger at not being able to work, the anxiety over work not done, the gas on the stomach. Dullest set of neurotic symptoms in the world, Trexler would think, as he obediently trudged back over them for the doctor's benefit. And then, having listened attentively to the recital, the doctor would spring his question: "Have you ever found anything that gives you relief?" And Trexler would answer, "Yes. A drink." And the doctor would nod his head knowingly.

As he became familiar with the pattern Trexler found that he increasingly tended to identify himself with the doctor, transferring himself into the doctor's seat — probably (he thought) some rather slick form of escapism. At any rate, it was nothing new for Trexler to identify himself with other people. Whenever he got into a cab, he instantly became the driver, saw everything from the hackman's angle (and the reaching over with the right hand, the nudging of the flag, the pushing it down, all the way down along the side of the meter), saw everything — traffic, fare, everything — through the eyes of Anthony Rocco, or Isidore Freedman, or Matthew Scott. In a barbershop, Trexler was the barber, his fingers curled around the comb, his hand on the tonic. Perfectly natural, then, that Trexler should soon be occupying the doctor's chair, asking the questions, waiting for the answers. He got quite interested in the doctor, in this way. He liked him, and he found him a not too difficult patient.

It was on the fifth visit, about halfway through, that the doctor turned to Trexler and said, suddenly, "What do you want?" He gave the word "want" special emphasis.

"I d'know," replied Trexler uneasily. "I guess nobody knows the answer to that one."

"Sure they do," replied the doctor.

"Do you know what you want?" asked Trexler narrowly.

"Certainly," said the doctor. Trexler noticed that at this point the doctor's chair slid slightly backward, away from him. Trexler stifled a small, internal smile. Scared as a rabbit, he said to himself. Look at him scoot!

"What *do* you want?" continued Trexler, pressing his advantage, pressing it hard.

The doctor glided back another inch away from his inquisitor. "I want a wing on the small house I own in Westport. I want more money, and more leisure to do the things I want to do."

Trexler was just about to say, "And what are those things you want to do, Doctor?" when he caught himself. Better not go too far, he mused. Better not lose possession of the ball. And besides, he thought, what the hell goes on here, anyway—me paying fifteen bucks a throw for these séances and then doing the work myself, asking the questions, weighing the answers. So he wants a new wing! There's a fine piece of theatrical gauze for you! A new wing.

Trexler settled down again and resumed the role of patient for the rest of the visit. It ended on a kindly, friendly note. The doctor reassured him that his fears were the cause of his sickness, and that his fears were unsubstantial. They shook hands, smiling.

Trexler walked dizzily through the empty waiting room and the doctor followed along to let him out. It was late; the secretary had shut up shop and gone home. Another day over the dam. "Goodbye," said Trexler. He stepped into the street, turned west toward Madison, and thought of the doctor all alone there, after hours, in that desolate hole—a man who worked longer hours than his secretary. Poor, scared, overworked bastard, thought Trexler. And that new wing!

It was an evening of clearing weather, the Park showing green and desirable in the distance, the last daylight applying a high lacquer to the brick and brownstone walls and giving the street scene a luminous and intoxicating splendor. Trexler meditated, as he walked, on what he wanted. "What do you want?" he heard again. Trexler knew what he wanted, and what, in general, all men wanted; and he was glad, in a way, that it was both inexpressible and unattainable, and that it wasn't a wing. He was satisfied to remember that it was deep, formless, enduring, and impossible of fulfillment, and that it made men sick, and that when you sauntered along Third Avenue and looked through the doorways into the dim saloons, you could sometimes pick out from the unregenerate ranks the ones who had not forgotten, gazing steadily into the bottoms of the glasses on the long chance that they could get another little peek at it. Trexler found himself renewed by the remembrance that what he wanted was at once great and microscopic, and that although it borrowed from the nature of large deeds and of youthful love and of old songs and early intimations, it was not any one of these things, and that it had not been isolated or pinned down, and that a man who attempted to define it in the privacy of a doctor's office would fall flat on his face.

Trexler felt invigorated. Suddenly his sickness seemed health, his dizziness stability. A small tree, rising between him and the light, stood there saturated with the evening, each gilt-edged leaf perfectly drunk with excellence and delicacy. Trexler's spine registered an ever so slight tremor as it picked up this natural disturbance in the lovely scene. "I want the second tree from the corner, just as it stands," he said, answering an imaginary question from an imaginary physician. And he felt a slow pride in realizing that what he wanted none could bestow, and that what he had none could take away. He felt content to be sick, unembarrassed at being afraid; and in the jungle of his fear he glimpsed (as he had so often glimpsed them before) the flashy tail feathers of the bird courage.

Then he thought once again of the doctor, and of his being left there all alone, tired, frightened. (The poor, scared guy, thought Trexler.) Trexler began humming "Moonshine Lullaby," his spirit reacting instantly to the hypodermic of Merman's healthy voice. He crossed Madison, boarded a downtown bus, and rode all the way to Fifty-second Street before he had a thought that could rightly have been called bizarre.

---

1. What symptoms does Trexler have?
2. What is the definition of the word *bizarre*? Give two or three examples of what might be considered "bizarre thoughts."
3. When Trexler reverses the roles and asks the doctor what *he* wants, what does he find out about the doctor? About himself? Why does he believe he is healthier than the doctor?
4. What would the doctor feel about the painting *Reservoir* (Plate III)? What would Trexler now feel about it? What standard is each applying?
5. Would you advise Trexler to quit his job and go fishing, like Nick in "Big Two-Hearted River"? Should the psychiatrist go fishing? Why? What would each get out of the experience, or fail to get out of it?
6. Which of the characters in this story is more like Morris Graves's *Blind Bird* (Plate IV)? Why?
7. Do you ever have any bizarre thoughts?

A Dream of Fair Women

KINGSLEY AMIS

The door still swinging to, and girls revive,
Aeronauts in the utmost altitudes
  Of boredom fainting, dive
In the bright oxygen of my nod;
Angels as well, a squadron of draped nudes,
  They roar towards their god.

Militant all, they fight to take my hat,
No more as yet; the other men retire
  Insulted, gestured at;
Each girl presses on me her share of what
Makes up the barn-door target of desire:
  And I am a crack shot.

Speech fails them, amorous, but each one's look,
Endorsed in other ways, begs me to sign
  Her body's autograph-book;
"Me first, Kingsley; I'm cleverest" each declares,
But no gourmet races downstairs to dine,
  Nor will I race upstairs.

Feigning aplomb, perhaps for half an hour,
I hover, and am shown by each princess
  The entrance to her tower;
Open, in that its tenant throws the key
At once to anyone, but not unless
  That anyone is me.

Now from the corridor their fathers cheer,
Their brothers, their young men; the cheers increase
  As soon as I appear;
From each I win a handshake and sincere
Congratulations; from the chief of police
  A nod, a wink, a leer.

A DREAM OF FAIR WOMEN From *A Case of Samples* by Kingsley Amis. Reprinted by permission of Curtis Brown Ltd., publishers.

This over, all delay is over too;
The first eight girls (the roster now agreed)
  Leap on me, and undo . . .
But honesty impels me to confess
That this is 'all a dream', which was, indeed,
  Not difficult to guess.

But wait; not 'just a dream', because, though good
And beautiful, it is also true, and hence
  Is rarely understood;
Who would choose any feasible ideal
In here and now's giant circumference,
  If that small room were real?

Only the best; the others find, have found
Love's ordinary distances too great,
  And eager, stand their ground;
Map-drunk explorers, dry-land sailors, they
See no arrival that can compensate
  For boredom on the way;

And, seeming doctrinaire, but really weak,
Limelighted dolls guttering in their brain,
  They come with me, to seek
The halls of theoretical delight,
The women of that ever-fresh terrain,
  The night after to-night.

---

1. Is Kingsley Amis describing a dream or a "daydream"? Why?
2. Would the psychiatrist in "The Second Tree from the Corner" classify this as a "bizzare thought?"
3. Is this a normal dream? Does Amis consider it a healthy dream? What is the difference between "normal" and "healthy"?
4. Amis catches himself entertaining this dream, records it, and evaluates it. What is his evaluation? What does he discover about himself?
5. Is Amis saying that egotism and sex are the primary motives of most of us? Is he saying that they are the best motives?
6. What do you believe are your primary motives? What do you really want most? Are most of your actions intelligently aimed at getting it?

---

1. What do you think the white tangle around the bird's feet represents?
2. What appears to be the most sensitive part of the bird's body? The least sensitive?
3. Is the bird capable of flight? Why not? Might it be capable of flights of the imagination?
4. What does the bird represent?
5. Do you think it knows that something is wrong with its life? What is wrong?

PLATE IV

BLIND BIRD: Morris Graves   Collection, The Museum of Modern Art, New York, 1940

Krahn

5

extending awareness

The miracles of nature are greater than those of the sky. If you will raise yourself to these, you will lift yourself above the skies. —*Pico della Mirandola*

In addition to what your senses can perceive within you and near you, there are all the things that you know to exist beyond your range. Some of these things you have seen; some you have seen pictures of or read about; some you know to exist through the discoveries of science.

Think of yourself as the center of a universe, and deliberately try to think of things around you that are far away—the place where you spent a vacation once, a city hundreds of miles away, another continent, a great star. Relate these things to your own central position, for you *are* the center of your own immense universe. Point to them: over there is the Pacific Ocean; that way Denver lies; down there is Africa; up there, the North Star. Think of these as part of you and you as part of them.

To be constantly aware of the great whole in which you exist is to cultivate stability and a sense of proportion. The unhappy person, the over-busy person, lives in the narrow cell of his own obsessions. The person who can laugh at his troubles is the person who, knowing that he is the center of his universe, knows also that his ego is not the whole universe. He is in contact with his whole environment, not just a part of it.

class exercise

Name and point to as many faraway things as you can think of. Try to describe briefly the feelings you have about each of them.

writing assignment

1. For one hour, write sentences that begin with such expressions as "above me," "below me," "five hundred miles to the west of me," "many light-years away from me out in space," etc. Strain your imagination thinking of real things, big and small, that are far away.
2. Use all of your senses: imagine the heat of tropical places and of the stars, the cold of Antarctica and of outer space, the force of ocean currents, the sounds of great cities, the odors of jungles and bazaars; identify with people and animals and plants. Put as much of this as you can into words. Let your imagination really roam!

class writing exercise

Choose a faraway place that you think of with pleasure; it may be a place you have seen, or it may be a place you have heard about, read about, or imagined.

Write a topic sentence about *why* you like to think about this place, and develop a paragraph around it. Give as vivid a picture as you can, full of specifics, so that your reader will share your feelings.

The Death Of Colonel Freeleigh

RAY BRADBURY

And then there is that day when all around, all around you hear the dropping of the apples, one by one, from the trees. At first it is one here and one there, and then it is three and then it is four and then nine and twenty, until the apples plummet like rain, fall like horse hoofs in the soft, darkening grass, and you are the last apple on the tree; and you wait for the wind to work you slowly free from your hold upon the sky, and drop you down and down. Long before you hit the grass you will have forgotten there ever was a tree, or other apples, or a summer, or green grass below. You will fall in darkness . . .

"No!"

Colonel Freeleigh opened his eyes quickly, sat erect in his wheel chair. He jerked his cold hand out to find the telephone. It was still there! He crushed it against his chest for a moment, blinking.

"I don't like that dream," he said to his empty room.

At last, his fingers trembling, he lifted the receiver and called the long-distance operator and gave her a number and waited, watching the bedroom door as if at any moment a plague of sons, daughters, grandsons, nurses, doctors, might swarm in to seize away this last vital luxury he permitted his failing senses. Many days, or was it years, ago, when his heart had thrust like a dagger through his ribs and flesh, he had heard the boys below . . . their names, what were they? Charles, Charlie, Chuck, yes! And Douglas! And Tom! He remembered! Calling his name far down the hall, but the door being locked in their faces, the boys turned away. You can't be excited, the doctor said. No visitors, no visitors, no visitors. And he heard the boys moving across the street, he saw them, he waved. And they waved back. "Colonel . . . Colonel . . ." And now he sat alone with the little gray toad of a heart flopping weakly here or there in his chest from time to time.

"Colonel Freeleigh," said the operator. "Here's your call. Mexico City. Erickson 3899."

And now the faraway but infinitely clear voice:

"Bueno."

"Jorge!" cried the old man.

"Señor Freeleigh! Again? This costs money."

"Let it cost! You know what to do."

"*Si.* The window?"

"The window, Jorge, if you please."

"A moment," said the voice.

And, thousands of miles away, in a southern land, in an office in a building in that land, there was the sound of footsteps retreating from the phone. The old man leaned forward, gripping the receiver tight to his wrinkled ear that ached with waiting for the next sound.

The raising of a window.

Ah, sighed the old man.

The sound of Mexico City on a hot yellow noon rose through the open window into the waiting phone. He could see Jorge standing there holding the mouthpiece out, out into the bright day.

"Señor . . ."

"No, no, please. Let me *listen.*"

He listened to the hooting of many metal horns, the squealing of brakes, the calls of vendors selling red-purple bananas and jungle oranges in their stalls. Colonel Freeleigh's feet began to move, hanging from the edge of his wheel chair, making the motions of a man walking. His eyes squeezed tight. He gave a series of immense sniffs, as if to gain the odors of meats hung on iron hooks in sunshine, cloaked with flies like a mantle of raisins; the smell of stone alleys wet with morning rain. He could feel the sun burn his spiny-bearded cheek, and he was twenty-five years old again, walking, walking, looking, smiling, happy to be alive, very much alert, drinking in colors and smells.

A rap on the door. Quickly he hid the phone under his lap robe.

The nurse entered. "Hello," she said. "Have you been good?"

"Yes." The old man's voice was mechanical. He could hardly see. The shock of a simple rap on a door was such that part of him was still in another city, far removed. He waited for his mind to rush home — it must be here to answer questions, act sane, be polite.

"I've come to check your pulse."

"Not now!" said the old man.

"You're not going anywhere, are you?" She smiled.

He looked at the nurse steadily. He hadn't been anywhere in ten years.

"Give me your wrist."

Her fingers, hard and precise, searched for the sickness in his pulse like a pair of calipers.

"What've you been doing to *excite* yourself?" she demanded.

"Nothing."

Her gaze shifted and stopped on the empty phone table. At that instant a horn sounded faintly, two thousand miles away.

She took the receiver from under the lap robe and held it before his face. "Why do you do this to yourself? You promised you wouldn't. That's how you hurt yourself in the first place, isn't it? Getting excited, talking too much. Those boys up here jumping around –"

"They sat quietly and listened," said the colonel. "And I told them things they'd never heard. The buffalo, I told them, the bison. It was worth it. I don't care. I was in a pure fever and I was alive. It doesn't matter if being so alive kills a man; it's better to have the quick fever every time. Now give me that phone. If you won't let the boys come up and sit politely I can at least talk to someone outside the room."

"I'm sorry, Colonel. Your grandson will have to know about this. I prevented his having the phone taken out last week. Now it looks like I'll let him go ahead."

"This is *my* house, my phone. I pay your salary!" he said.

"To make you well, not get you excited." She wheeled his chair across the room. "To bed with you now, young man!"

From bed he looked back at the phone and kept looking at it.

"I'm going to the store for a few minutes," the nurse said. "Just to be sure you don't use the phone again, I'm hiding your wheel chair in the hall."

She wheeled the empty chair out the door. In the downstairs entry, he heard her pause and dial the extension phone.

Was she phoning Mexico City? he wondered. She wouldn't dare!

The front door shut.

He thought of the last week here, alone, in his room, and the secret, narcotic calls across continents, an isthmus, whole jungle countries of rain forest, blue-orchid plateaus, lakes and hills . . . talking . . . talking . . . to Buenos Aires . . . and . . . Lima . . . Rio de Janeiro . . . .

He lifted himself in the cool bed. Tomorrow the telephone gone! What a greedy fool he had been! He slipped his brittle ivory legs down from the bed, marveling at their desiccation. They seemed to be things which had been fastened to his body while he slept one night, while his younger legs were taken off and burned in the cellar furnace. Over the years, they had destroyed all of him, removing hands, arms, and legs and leaving him with substitutes as delicate and useless as chess pieces. And now they were tampering with something more intangible – the memory; they were trying to cut the wires which led back into another year.

He was across the room in a stumbling run. Grasping the phone, he took it with him as he slid down the wall to sit upon the floor. He got the long-distance operator, his heart exploding within him, faster and faster, a blackness in his eyes. "Hurry, hurry!"

He waited.

"Bueno?"

"Jorge, we were cut off."

"You must not phone again, Señor," said the faraway voice. "Your nurse called me. She says you are very ill. I must hang up."

"No, Jorge! Please!" the old man pleaded. "One last time, listen to me. They're taking the phone out tomorrow. I can never call you again."

Jorge said nothing.

The old man went on. "For the love of God, Jorge! For friendship, then, for the old days! You don't know what it means. You're my age, but you can *move!* I haven't moved anywhere in ten years."

He dropped the phone and had trouble picking it up, his chest was so thick with pain. "Jorge! You *are* still there, aren't you?"

"This will be the last time?" said Jorge.

"I promise!"

The phone was laid on a desk thousands of miles away. Once more, with that clear familiarity, the footsteps, the pause, and, at last, the raising of the window.

"Listen," whispered the old man to himself.

And he heard a thousand people in another sunlight, and the faint, tinkling music of an organ grinder playing "La Marimba" — oh, a lovely, dancing tune.

With eyes tight, the old man put up his hand as if to click pictures of an old cathedral, and his body was heavier with flesh, younger, and he felt the hot pavement underfoot.

He wanted to say, "You're still there, aren't you? All of you people in that city in the time of the early siesta, the shops closing, the little boys crying *loteria nacional para hoy!* to sell lottery tickets. You are all there, the people in the city. I can't believe I was ever among you. When you are away from a city it becomes a fantasy. Any town, New York, Chicago, with its people, becomes improbable with distance. Just as I am improbable here, in Illinois, in a small town by a quiet lake. All of us improbable to one another because we are not present to one another. And so it is good to hear the sounds, and know that Mexico City is still there and the people moving and living . . ."

He sat with the receiver tightly pressed to his ear.

And at last, the clearest, most improbable sound of all — the sound of a green trolley car going around a corner — a trolley burdened with brown and alien and beautiful people, and the sound of other people running and calling out with triumph as they leaped up and swung aboard and vanished around a corner on the shrieking rails and were borne away in the sun-blazed distance to leave only the sound of *tortillas* frying on the market stoves, or was it merely the ever rising and falling hum and burn of static quivering along two thousand miles of copper wire . . .

The old man sat on the floor.

Time passed.

A downstairs door opened slowly. Light footsteps came in, hesitated, then ventured up the stairs. Voices murmered.

"We shouldn't be here!"

"He phoned me, I tell you. He needs visitors bad. We can't let him down."

"He's sick!"

"Sure! But he said to come when the nurse's out. We'll only stay a second, say hello, and . . ."

The door to the bedroom moved wide. The three boys stood looking in at the old man seated there on the floor.

"Colonel Freeleigh?" said Douglas softly.

There was something in his silence that made them all shut up their mouths.

They approached, almost on tiptoe.

Douglas, bent down, disengaged the phone from the old man's now quite cold fingers. Douglas lifted the receiver to his own ear, listened. Above the static he heard a strange, a far, a final sound.

Two thousand miles away, the closing of a window.

---

1. What does the nurse fail to realize about her patient? What gives him the "will to live"?
2. What is the meaning of the window? Why does it close at the end?
3. What are some of your own "windows" that make your life worth living?
4. What things does Colonel Freeleigh value most? Why?
5. Colonel Freeleigh's "window" lets in only sounds, but the sounds suggest many kinds of perceptions. What are some of them?

"Morning Song" from Senlin

CONRAD AIKEN

It is morning, Senlin says, and in the morning
When the light drips through the shutters like the dew,
I arise, I face the sunrise,
And do the things my fathers learned to do.
Stars in the purple dusk above the rooftops
Pale in a saffron mist and seem to die,
And I myself on a swiftly tilting planet
Stand before a glass and tie my tie.

Vine-leaves tap my window,
Dew-drops sing to the garden stones,
The robin chirps in the chinaberry tree
Repeating three clear tones.

It is morning. I stand by the mirror
And tie my tie once more.
While waves far off in a pale rose twilight
Crash on a coral shore.
I stand by a mirror and comb my hair:
How small and white my face! —
The green earth tilts through a sphere of air
And bathes in a flame of space.
There are houses hanging above the stars
And stars hung under a sea.
And a sun far off in a shell of silence
Dapples my walls for me.

It is morning, Senlin says, and in the morning
Should I not pause in the light to remember god?
Uupright and firm I stand on a star unstable,
He is immense and lonely as a cloud.

I will dedicate this moment before my mirror
To him alone, for him I will comb my hair.
Accept these humble offerings, cloud of silence!
I will think of you as I descend the stair.

Vine-leaves tap my window,
The snail-track shines on the stones,
Dew-drops flash from the chinaberry tree
Repeating two clear tones.

It is morning, I awake from a bed of silence,
Shining I rise from the starless waters of sleep.
The walls are about me still as in the evening,
I am the same, and the same name still I keep.
The earth revolves with me, yet makes no motion,
The stars pale silently in a coral sky.
In a whistling void I stand before my mirror,
Unconcerned, and tie my tie.

There are horses neighing on far-off hills
Tossing their long white manes,
And mountains flash in the rose-white dusk,
Their shoulders black with rains.

It is morning. I stand by the mirror
And surprise my soul once more;
The blue air rushes above my ceiling,
There are suns beneath my floor.

. . . It is morning, Senlin says, I ascend from darkness
And depart on the winds of space for I know not where,
My watch is wound, a key is in my pocket,
And the sky is darkened as I descend the stair.
There are shadows across the windows, clouds in heaven,
And a god among the stars; and I will go
Thinking of him as I might think of daybreak
And humming a tune I know.

Vine-leaves tap at the window,
Dew-drops sing to the garden stones,
The robin chirps in the chinaberry tree
Repeating three clear tones.

1. What is Senlin's attitude toward the immensity and variety of things around him? Try to find one word which will adequately describe this feeling.
2. Which senses does he use?
3. What similarities do you find between Senlin's universe and Colonel Freeleigh's? What differences? Which one is less dependent upon material possessions? Upon memories?
4. Conrad Aiken perceives things somewhat differently from William Carlos Williams, the poet of "The Great Figure" (Unit 2). What sort of thing does Williams seem to notice that Aiken does not, and vice versa?

---

1. Van Gogh is communicating an intense awareness of the moon and stars, the hills and trees and sleeping town. What feeling does the picture give you toward these things?
2. What aspect or quality of these things do you think Van Gogh feels most strongly?
3. How does his feeling differ from that of Aiken in "Morning Song" from *Senlin*? From that of Hemingway in "Big Two-Hearted River" (Unit 1)?
4. See if you can express in one sentence what Van Gogh seems to be saying about the universe.

PLATE V THE STARRY NIGHT: Vincent van Gogh Collection, The Museum of Modern Art, New York: acquired through the Lillie P. Bliss Bequest

6

observing a person

> We usually see only the things we are looking for — so much that we sometimes see them where they are not.
>
> —*Eric Hoffer*

A psychologist named Dr. Robert Coles worked for several years with white and black children in New Orleans, where school integration was slowly taking place against angry opposition. In order to find out the children's attitudes toward race relations, he asked them to draw pictures. In an article in *Atlantic Monthly* called "When I Draw the Lord He'll Be a Real Big Man," Dr. Coles first tells how a black girl named Ruby sees her classmates; then he goes on to tell about a white boy, Jimmie:

Ruby had a classmate for several years named Jimmie, a lively, agile particularly freckled boy whose blond hair tended to fall over his forehead. When I first asked Ruby to draw a picture of any school chum she wished (there were only three at the time), she obliged with a picture of Jimmie. "He is a good boy, sometimes," she commented, adding the last word of qualification after a genuine moment of hesitancy. In point of fact, Jimmie's behavior troubled her. One minute he would be attentive and generous, anxious to play games or even share food with her. Yet in a flash he could turn on her, and not just as one child will do with another. Ruby knew why, and could put it into words: "Jimmie plays with me OK, but then he remembers that I'm colored, so he gets bad."

I asked whether he was "bad" at other times — fresh or spiteful simply out of a moment's impulse. She handled my question rather forthrightly, even with a touch of impatience: "Well, he's bad sometimes when he wants things his own way and someone won't let him get it; but I mean it's different when he gets bad because I'm colored. He can be my friend and play real nice with me, and suddenly he just turns and says bad things, and he even gets scared of me and says he's going to leave; but he comes back. He forgets, and then he remembers again."

Jimmie's parents had it no easier. Like him they could not establish in their minds a clear-cut set of attitudes toward colored people. When riots made their son's school attendance dangerous, they kept him home. As the mobs achieved their purpose, a near-total boycott, the noise they made and the terror they inspired in passersby gradually subsided. A few white families sent their children back to the schools involved, some in direct defiance of the small crowds that persisted, others rather quietly, almost secretly, through rear doors or side doors. Jimmie's parents sent him back as soon as it was safe to do so. When I saw him come to the school, neatly dressed, carrying his lunch box, I thought the very spirit of sanity resided in him, and with him was returning to the deserted halls and classrooms of the building he so casually and confidently entered. There was something very open and calm about him as he walked along, and I guessed something refreshing, something unsullied also.

As I came to know Jimmie and his family I realized how unfair I had been to the boy when I first saw him. I pictured him as Ruby's hope. In fact, he returned to school in spite of Ruby because his parents did not want him to waste months of time learning nothing. When he first met Ruby, he told her the facts rather explicitly: "My mother told me to stay away from you." Ruby told me what he had said, then informed me that Jimmie had contradicted his own words seconds later by asking her to join him in a game. "So I did" was her way of letting the matter drop.

When Jimmie and I started drawing together, he made his feelings about Negroes rather clear: either they were in some fashion related to animals, or the color of their skin proved that if they were human they were certainly dirty human beings — dangerous, too. I don't think Ruby ever knew the fear she inspired in Jimmie, nor did Jimmie have any idea how very much Ruby strived to portray herself with his features and coloring, as if then she could be less afraid of *him.*

For a while Jimmie drew pictures of his home, his parents, his friends, and himself. He was particularly fond of landscapes, and once did eight of them in two weeks, each surprisingly different, though all dwelling upon trees, grass, and water. When I first asked him to draw a picture of Ruby, he looked at me quite in dismay and said he couldn't. I asked why. He now appeared cross: "Because I don't know what she looks like. I don't look at her close if I can help it."

I asked him whether sometimes he couldn't help noticing her. "Accidents happen sometimes, Jimmie; even when we try to do as we feel we should." He nodded, and allowed that he had managed a few glimpses at Ruby, and would try to draw her. He started to do so rather furtively, then somehow lost his nervousness, so that by the end he was the confident and scrupulously attentive craftsman and landscapist he always was — except, that is, for what he had done to Ruby. It was almost as if he had suddenly embraced surrealism. In the midst of a stretch of grass he abruptly placed her, without feet, legs inserted in a piece of land left strangely sandy and barren in contrast to what surrounded it. He made Ruby small, though her arms were larger proportionately than those he usually drew. She had the thinnest line of a mouth and pinpoint eyes. Her hair was frizzy black, yet curiously and inappropriately long. She was brown-black, much more strikingly so than Ruby's medium brown complexion justified.

After a while Jimmie was able to develop on paper the various conflicting feelings he had toward Ruby and her race. He drew Ruby many times, at intervals upon my request and often because he wanted to do so, or felt that I wished him to do so. Jimmie had obvious trouble picturing her at all. He hesitated as he did at no other time. For many weeks she appeared only as a speck of brown, or in caricature. He told me that he didn't know what she looked like: "She's funny. She's not like us, so I can't draw her like my friends. Besides, she hides a lot from us." When I asked him where she hid, he said, "She doesn't really hide. I mean she stays away sometimes; but if I say something, she answers me all right."

I wanted to know whether he had any idea why Ruby might be keeping her distance from him and the others. He knew exactly why: "Well, she's colored, that's why." I reminded Jimmie that colored children lived nearby, and often played with white children. In New Orleans large areas of the city are thoroughly mixed racially, and have been for generations. He knew that, too: "That's different. It's on the street, not in school. My daddy says that on the street it's for everybody, but inside is where you have to be careful."

When I asked him whether he would draw a picture of Ruby at school, he readily obliged, though invariably he put Ruby in the play area outside the building. Finally I mentioned what I saw him doing, and he scarcely hesitated before replying: "The teacher said it won't be long before we go back to normal. She said that if most kids still stay home and the people still make all the noise in front of the school, then they'll send Ruby away and the trouble will be over; she said Ruby still isn't a regular member of the school, but that we have to be polite, anyway." The yard, for him, was like a waiting room, and in one drawing he put a bench in it — in actuality there was none — and he put Ruby on the bench.

In time Jimmie took Ruby into the building he drew, and in time he regularly came to see her as an individual. Amorphous spots and smudges of brown slowly took on form and structure. Ruby began to look human every time, rather than, say, like a rodent or a fallen leaf one day and a rather deformed human being the next. Eventually she gained eyes and well-formed ears. It took more time for her to obtain a normal mouth; and only after a year of knowing her would Jimmie credit her with the pretty clothes he often gave to other girls. In describing Ruby's speech after he had finished his pictures, Jimmie for a long time tried his best to render his version of a Negro dialect. His parents began enjoying such performances, and also hearing from him how "the nigra" was doing in school. *They* were changing, too — from calling Ruby a "nigger" to calling her a "nigra," and from wanting no mention of her at home to insisting upon information about her schoolwork and her general behavior. By the middle of our second year's talks Jimmie was forgetting himself and telling me in his own words and accents what Ruby might be saying in one of his productions.

Jimmie may have tried to ignore Ruby, he may have consigned her to anonymity, even to the indignity of a dot, or an animal-like appearance, but he never really overlooked the difference her presence made to his school. He showed how embattled it was by a policeman here, a picket with a sign there. The demonstrators were drawn big and openmouthed, their arms unusually beefy, their hands prominent indeed, a child's view of the shrill, stifling, clutching power they exercised over the school's population. As they gradually lost that power and began to disband, Jimmie pictured them smaller.

The school building itself took on a variety of shapes in Jimmie's mind and on his paper. At first it was a confusing, almost ramshackle building, its walls as flimsy and unreliable as the school's future seemed at the time. Slowly, though, Jimmie realized that, as he put it, "We're going to make it." Quite casually, without self-consciousness, he showed that he meant what he said. His school grew in size, each time looking sounder and more attractive for all the wear it was taking from its assailants. Eventually he allowed the building to dominate everything around it, from the shrubbery to the crowd of human beings who once impressed both him and Ruby with their persistence and assertiveness.

Although Dr. Coles's example is an extreme one, we can guess that we are all a little like Jimmie in some ways: that limited upbringing and experience have left us with some pretty big "blank spots" or distorted areas in our perception, especially our perception of people. Jimmie is like the woman in "Arrangement in Black and White." Although he has perfectly good eyesight and hearing, he does not see or hear Ruby at first. As he begins to become aware of her, his impressions are distorted; and finally, after more than a year of association, he begins to see her as she is. Possibly you have had such an experience of "seeing someone for the first time." Possibly you still have some such experiences ahead of you.

In observing a person, the first step is to *look* at him closely, noting the *facts*, making only reasonable *inferences*, and refraining from opinions.

A *fact* is a direct observation of the senses which cannot be disputed, as, "She is wearing a diamond ring on the third finger of her left hand." An *inference* is a conclusion about something you cannot observe directly but which the facts lead you to believe, as, "She is probably engaged or wants others to think she is." (If you have forgotten what an *opinion* is, review the Introduction.)

class exercise

Turn your seat to face the person next to you. (If the class is odd-numbered, three can work together.) Try to describe him in such a way that your reader could recognize him in a crowd of strangers, even if he changed his clothing and the color of his hair.

writing assignment

1. Taking a small notebook with you, go to some public place such as a bus or railway station, a city bus, a crowded supermarket, or a dime store: a place where you can take notes without being too conspicuous.
2. Pick out a person who looks interesting, preferably an older person, one who is unlike most of the older people you know. Observe him as closely as you can without attracting attention.
3. Take detailed notes about your subject. First, write down a general description such as you would give someone who was looking for him. Then do the detective work: catalogue every detail you can observe from which some inference might be made about the subject's occupation, financial status, family status, personal habits, home life, and so on.
4. Now, putting your material in the kind of order you used in the writing assignment in Unit 1, make up an intensive description of the person, including all of your sound inferences and the evidence to support them.

class writing exercise

Rewrite the material you have collected in the writing assignment, organizing it into paragraphs with topic sentences.

Begin with a paragraph of general description. The topic sentence should reflect the general impression the person gives at first glance, as, "He is a tall, neatly dressed man who probably works indoors." Then round out the paragraph with the fundamental physical facts that support this generalization, such as height, weight, complexion, and so on.

Then, using your inferences as topic sentences, write two or three more paragraphs about such matters as the details of his dress and appearance, his movements and facial expressions, his reactions to things around him. Try to *unify* each paragraph by putting in only material which supports the inference; and try to give full and convincing evidence for each inference.

Unity is sticking to your subject. A *unified* paragraph is one in which every sentence is devoted to proving the generalization in the topic sentence.

from The Ram in the Thicket

WRIGHT MORRIS

He turned slowly on the bed, careful to keep the springs quiet, and as he lowered his feet he scooped his socks from the floor. As a precaution Mother had slept the first few months of their marriage in her corset — as a precaution and as an aid to self-control. In the fall they had ordered twin beds. Carrying his shoes — today, of all days, would be a trial for Mother — he tiptoed to the closet and picked up his shirt and pants. There was simply no reason, as he had explained to her twenty years ago, why she should get up when he could just as well get a bite for himself. He had made that suggestion when the boy was just a baby and she needed her strength. Even as it was she didn't come out of it any too well. The truth was, Mother was so thorough about everything she did that her breakfasts usually took an hour or more. When he did it himself he was out of the kitchen in ten, twelve minutes and without leaving any pile of dishes around. By himself he could quick-rinse them in a little hot water, but with Mother there was the dish pan and all of the suds. Mother had the

---

idea that a meal simply wasn't a meal without setting the table and using half the dishes in the place. It was easier to do it himself, and except for Sunday, when they had brunch, he was out of the house an hour before she got up. He had a bite of lunch at the store and at four o'clock he did the day's shopping since he was right downtown anyway. There was a time he called her up and inquired as to what she thought she wanted, but since he did all the buying he knew that better himself. As secretary for the League of Women Voters she had enough on her mind in times like these without cluttering it up with food. Now that he left the store an hour early he usually got home in the midst of her nap or while she was taking her bath. As he had nothing else to do he prepared the vegetables, and dressed the meat, as Mother had never shown much of a flair for meat. There had been a year — when the boy was small and before he had taken up that gun — when she had made several marvelous lemon meringue pies. But feeling as she did about the gun — and she told them both how she felt about it — she didn't see why she should slave in the kitchen for people like that. She always spoke to them as *they* — or as *you* plural — from the time he had given the boy the gun. Whether this was because they were both men, both culprits, or both something else, they were never entirely separate things again. When she called *they* would both answer, and though the boy had been gone two years he still felt him *there,* right beside him, when Mother said *you.*

For some reason he could not understand — although the rest of the house was as neat as a pin, too neat — the room they *lived* in was always a mess. Mother refused to let the cleaning woman set her foot in it. Whenever she left the house she locked the door. Long, long ago he had said something, and she had said something, and she had said she had wanted one room in the house where she could relax and just let her hair down. That had sounded so wonderfully human, so unusual for Mother, that he had been completely taken with it. As a matter of fact he still didn't know what to say. It was the only room in the house — except for the screened-in porch in the summer — where he could take off his shoes and open his shirt on his underwear. If the room was *clean,* it would be clean like all of the others, and that would leave him nothing but the basement and the porch. The way the boy took to the out-of-doors — he stopped looking for his cuff links, began to look for pins — was partially because he couldn't find a place in the house to sit down. They had just redecorated the house — the boy at that time was just a little shaver — and Mother had spread newspapers over everything. There hadn't been a chair in the place — except the straight-backed ones at the table — that hadn't been, that *wasn't* covered with a piece of newspaper. Anyone who had ever scrunched around on a paper knew what that was like. It was at that time that he had got the idea of having his pipe in the basement, reading in the bedroom, and the boy had taken to the out-of-doors. Because he had always wanted a gun himself, and because the boy was alone, with no kids around to play with, he had brought him home that damn gun. A thousand-shot gun by the name of Daisy — funny that he should remember the name — and five thousand bee-bees in a drawstring canvas bag.

That gun had been a mistake — he began to shave himself in tepid, lukewarm water rather than let it run hot, which would bang the pipes and wake Mother up. That gun had been a mistake — when the telegram came that the boy had been killed Mother hadn't said a word, but she made it clear whose fault it was. There was never any doubt, *any* doubt, as to just whose fault it was.

He stopped thinking while he shaved, attentive to the mole at the edge of his mustache, and leaned to the mirror to avoid dropping suds on the rug. There had been a time when he had wondered about an oriental throw rug in the bathroom, but over twenty years he had become accustomed to it. As a matter of fact he sort of missed it whenever they had guests with children and Mother remembered to take it up. Without the rug he always felt just a little uneasy, a little naked, in the bathroom, and this made him whistle or turn on the water and let it run. If it hadn't been for that he might not have noticed as soon as he did that Mother did the same thing whenever anybody was in the house. She turned on the water and let it run until she was through with the toilet, then she would flush it before she turned the water off. If you happen to have old-fashioned plumbing, and have lived with a person for twenty years, you can't help noticing little things like that. He had got to be a little like that himself: since the boy had gone he used the one in the basement or waited until he got down to the store. As a matter of fact it was more convenient, didn't wake Mother up, and he could have his pipe while he was sitting there.

With his pants on, but carrying his shirt — for he might get it soiled preparing breakfast — he left the bathroom and tiptoed down the stairs.

Although the boy had gone, was gone, that is, Mother still liked to preserve her slip covers and the kitchen linoleum. It was a good piece, well worth preserving, but unless there were guests in the house he never saw it — he nearly forgot that it was there. The truth was he had to look at it once a week, every time he put down the papers — but right now he couldn't tell you what color that linoleum was! He couldn't do it, and wondering what in the world color it was he bent over and peeked at it — blue. Blue and white, Mother's favorite colors of course.

Suddenly he felt the stirring in his bowels. Usually this occurred while he was rinsing the dishes after his second cup of coffee or after the first long draw on his pipe. He was not supposed to smoke in the morning, but it was more important to be regular that way than regular with his pipe. Mother had been the first to realize this — not in so many words — but she would rather he did anything than not be able to do *that.*

He measured out a pint and a half of water, put it over a medium fire, and added just a pinch of salt. Then he walked to the top of the basement stairs, turned on the light, and at the bottom turned it off. He dipped his head to pass beneath a sagging line of wash, the sleeves dripping, and with his hands out, for the corner was dark, he entered the cell.

The basement toilet had been put in to accommodate the help, who had to use something, and Mother would not have them on her oriental rug. Until the day he dropped some money out of his pants and had to strike a match to look for it, he had never noticed what kind of stool it was. Mother had picked it up secondhand — she had never told him where — because she couldn't see buying something new for a place always in the dark. It was very old, with a chain pull, and operated on a principle that invariably produced quite a splash. But in spite of that, he preferred it to the one at the store and very much more than the one upstairs. This was rather hard to explain since the seat was pretty cold in the winter and the water sometimes nearly froze. But it was private like no other room in the house. Considering that the house was as good as empty, that was a strange thing to say, but it was the only way to say how he felt. If he went off for a walk like the boy, Mother would miss him, somebody would see him, and he wouldn't feel right about it anyhow. All he wanted was a dark quiet place and the feeling that for five minutes, just five minutes, nobody would be looking for him. Who would ever believe five minutes like that were so hard to come by? The closest he had ever been to the boy — after he had given him the gun — was the morning he had found him here on the stool. It was then that the boy had said, *et tu, Brutus,* and they had both laughed so hard they had had to hold their sides. The boy had put his head in a basket of wash so Mother wouldn't hear. Like everything the boy said there were two or three ways to take it, and in the dark Mr. Ormsby could not see his face. When he stopped laughing the boy said, *Well Pop, I suppose one flush ought to do,* but Mr. Ormsby had not been able to say anything. To be called Pop made him so weak that he had to sit right down on the stool, just like he was, and support his head in his hands. Just as he had never had a name for the boy, the boy had never had a name for him — none, that is, that Mother would permit him to use. Of all the names Mother couldn't stand, Pop was the worst, and he agreed with her, it was vulgar, common, and used by strangers to intimidate old men. He agreed with her, completely — until he heard the word in the boy's mouth. It was only natural that the boy would use it if he ever had the chance — but he never dreamed that any word, especially *that* word, could mean what it did. It made him weak, he had to sit down and pretend he was going about his business, and what a blessing it was that the place was dark. Nothing more was said, ever, but it remained their most important conversation — so important they were afraid to try and improve on it. Days later he remembered the rest of the boy's sentence, and how shocking it was but without any *sense* of shock. A blow so sharp that he had no sense of pain, only a knowing, as he had under gas, that he had been worked on. For two, maybe three minutes, there in the dark they had been what Mother called them, they were *they* — and they were there in the basement because they were so much alike. When the telegram came, and when he knew what he would find, he had brought it there, had struck a match, and read what it said. The match filled the cell with light and he saw — he couldn't help seeing — piles of tin goods in the space beneath the stairs. Several dozen cans of tuna fish and salmon, and since *he* was the one that had the points, bought the groceries, there was only one place Mother could have got such things. It had been a greater shock than the telegram — that was the honest-to-God's truth and anyone who knew Mother as well as he did would have felt the same. It was unthinkable, but there it was — and there were more on top of the water closet, where he peered while precariously balanced on the stool. Cans of pineapple, crabmeat, and tins of Argentine beef. He had been stunned, the match had burned down and actually scorched his fingers, and he nearly killed himself when he forgot and stepped off the seat. Only later in the morning — after he had sent the flowers to ease the blow for Mother — did he realize how such a thing *must* have occurred. Mother knew so many influential people, and before the war they gave her so much, that they had very likely given her all of this stuff as well. Rather than turn it down and needlessly alienate people, influential people, Mother had done the next best thing. While the war was on she refused to serve it, or profiteer in any way — and at the same time not alienate people foolishly. It had been an odd thing, certainly, that he should discover all of that by the same match that he read the telegram. Naturally, he never breathed a word of it to Mother, as something like that, even though she was not superstitious, would really upset her. It was one of those things that he and the boy would keep to themselves.

It would be like Mother to think of putting it in here, the very last place that the cleaning woman would look for it. The new cleaning woman would neither go upstairs nor down, and did whatever she did somewhere else. Mr. Ormsby lit a match to see if everything was all right — hastily blew it out when he saw that the can pile had increased. He stood up — then hurried up the stairs without buttoning his pants as he could hear the water boiling. He added half a cup, then measured three heaping tablespoons of coffee into the bottom of the double boiler, buttoned his pants. Looking at his watch he saw that it was seven-thirty-five. As it would be a hard day — sponsoring a boat was a man-sized job — he would give Mother another ten minutes or so. He took two bowls from the cupboard, sat them on blue pottery saucers, and with the grapefruit knife in his hand walked to the icebox.

As he put his head in the icebox door — in order to see he had to — Mr. Ormsby stopped breathing and closed his eyes. What had been dying for some time was now dead. He leaned back, inhaled, leaned in again. The floor of the icebox was covered with a fine assortment of jars full of leftovers Mother simply could not throw away. Some of the jars were covered with little oilskin hoods, some with saucers, and some with paper snapped on with a rubber band. It was impossible to tell, from the outside, which one it was. Seating himself on the floor he removed them one at a time, starting at the front and working toward the back. As he had done this many times before, he got well into the problem, near the middle, before troubling to sniff anything. A jar which might have been carrots — it was hard to tell without probing — was now a furry marvel of green mold. It smelled only mildly, however, and Mr. Ormsby remembered that this was penicillin, the life-giver. A spoonful of cabbage — it had been three months since they had had cabbage — had a powerful stench but was still not the one he had in mind. There were two more jars of mold, the one screwed tight he left alone as it had a frosted look and the top of the lid bulged. The culprit, however, was not there at all, but in an open saucer on the next shelf — part of an egg — Mr. Ormsby had beaten the white himself. He placed the saucer on the sink and returned all but two of the jars to the icebox; the cabbage and the explosive looking one. If it smelled he took it out, otherwise Mother had to see for herself as she refused to take *their* word for these things. When he was just a little shaver the boy had walked into the living room full of Mother's guests and showed them something in a jar. Mother had been horrified — but she naturally thought it a frog or something and not a bottle out of her own icebox. When one of the ladies asked the boy where in the world he had found it, he naturally said, *In the icebox*. Mother had never forgiven him. After that she forbade him to look in the box without permission, and the boy had not so much as peeked in it since. He would eat only what he found on the table, or ready to eat in the kitchen — or what he found at the end of those walks he took everywhere.

With the jar of cabbage and furry mold Mr. Ormsby made a trip to the garage, picked up the garden spade, walked around behind. At one time he had emptied the jars and merely buried the contents, but recently, since the war that is, he had buried it all. Part of it was a question of time — he had more work to do at the store — but the bigger part of it was to put an end to the jars. Not that it worked out that way — all Mother had to do was open a new one — but it gave him a real satisfaction to bury them. Now that the boy and his dogs were gone there was simply no one around the house to eat up all the food Mother saved.

There were worms in the fork of earth he had turned and he stood looking at them — *they* both had loved worms — when he remembered the water boiling on the stove. He dropped everything and ran, ran right into Emil Ludlow, the milkman, before he noticed him. Still on the run he went up the steps and through the screen door into the kitchen — he was clear to the stove before he remembered the door would slam. He started back, but too late, and in the silence that followed the BANG he stood with his eyes tightly closed, his fists clenched. Usually he remained in this condition until a sign from Mother — a thump on the floor or her voice at the top of the stairs. None came, however, only the sound of the milk bottles that Emil Ludlow was leaving on the porch. Mr. Ormsby gave him time to get away, waited until he heard the horse walking, then he went out and brought the milk in. At the icebox he remembered the water — why it was he had come running in the first place — and he left the door open and hurried to the stove. It was down to half a cup but not, thank heavens, dry. He added a full pint, then returned and put the milk in the icebox; took out the butter, four eggs, and a Flori-gold grapefruit. Before he cut the grapefruit he looked at his watch and seeing that it was ten minutes to eight, an hour before train time, he opened the stairway door.

"Ohhh Mother!" he called, and then he returned to the grapefruit.

---

1. Instead of describing Mrs. Ormsby directly, Wright Morris has chosen to introduce her entirely through bits of evidence in her environment, from which the reader makes *inferences*. (Her husband, of course, is part of the environment.) What are several of these bits of evidence?
2. What inferences do you make from them?
3. After the screen door banged, Mr. Ormsby "stood with his eyes tightly closed, his fists clenched." Why?
4. See if you can make some general statements about Mrs. Ormsby's character. What are her chief motivations? What things does she value most in life?
5. Could you use description of the environment to tell about a person in your family? See if you can think of some details in your home that would tell us about the character of someone who lives there.
6. What parts of her environment is Mrs. Ormsby in contact with? What parts is she unaware of?

Ex-Basketball Player

JOHN UPDIKE

Pearl Avenue runs past the high school lot,
Bends with the trolley tracks, and stops, cut off
Before it has a chance to go two blocks,
At Colonel McComsky Plaza. Berth's Garage
Is on the corner facing west, and there,
Most days, you'll find Flick Webb, who helps Berth out.

Flick stands tall among the idiot pumps —
Five on a side, the old bubble-head style,
Their rubber elbows hanging loose and low.
One's nostrils are two S's, and his eyes
An E and O. And one is squat, without
A head at all — more of a football type.

Once, Flick played for the high school team, the Wizards.
He was good: in fact, the best. In '46,
He bucketed three hundred ninety points,
A county record still. The ball loved Flick.
I saw him rack up thirty-eight or forty
In one home game. His hands were like wild birds.

He never learned a trade; he just sells gas,
Checks oil, and changes flats. Once in a while,
As a gag, he dribbles an inner tube,
But most of us remember anyway.
His hands are fine and nervous on the lug wrench.
It makes no difference to the lug wrench, though.

Off work, he hangs around Mae's Luncheonette.
Grease-grey and kind of coiled, he plays pinball,
Sips lemon cokes, and smokes those thin cigars;
Flick seldom speaks to Mae, just sits and nods
Beyond her face towards the bright applauding tiers
Of Necco Wafers, Nibs, and Juju Beads.

---

1. John Updike has written about certain features of Flick's life and has left out others. What are some of the things he has *not* told us about Flick?
2. What *inferences* does he lead you to make? What *opinions* does he seem to want you to form?
3. What do the first three lines about Pearl Avenue suggest about Flick's job? Has Flick, too, "bent with the tracks"? In what way?
4. What are the pumps used to suggest? Why does the poet call their hoses "rubber elbows hanging loose and low"? What is the *analogy* here? What does it help to make clear?
5. How does Flick differ from Nick in "Big Two-Hearted River"? From Colonel Freeleigh?
6. Do you think it would do Flick any good to go fishing, like Nick? Why or why not?
7. What are some specific parts of his environment that Flick has lost contact with?

---

1. At first glance, you might have the impression that Grant Wood has portrayed these two people "exactly as they are." But look more closely. In what ways does this painting differ from a photograph?
2. By the way in which he has painted the picture, the artist has tried to lead you to certain inferences and opinions about the couple. Why has he posed them in this position?
3. What has he emphasized in painting their clothing?
4. What things has he chosen to show in the background? What impression is he trying to give by these choices? Is he using environment to tell about character, like Wright Morris in "The Ram in the Thicket"?
5. What are some of the things he has left out? Why?
6. Imagine yourself a relative of these people, visiting them in their home. What qualities of their characters would help to make your stay pleasant? Unpleasant? On what evidence do you base these inferences? Would some of your pleasure or displeasure have to do with your own emotional attitudes? Which attitudes?

PLATE VI

AMERICAN GOTHIC: Grant Wood   The Art Institute of Chicago

Drawing by Chas. Addams; © 1939, 1967 The New Yorker Magazine, Inc.

7

evaluating possessions

Before we set our hearts too much upon anything, see how happy those are who already possess it. —*La Rochefoucauld*

What do you mean when you say an object "belongs" to you? Pass over such obvious answers as "I paid for it," or "I have a piece of paper that says it's mine." What is the relationship between you and the thing? What does it mean to you, and what do you mean to it?

A thing may be valued because it performs a useful service, like a jackknife or a warm coat. But values are frequently assigned to things in arbitrary ways. Objects are often *symbols*: a *symbol* is something that stands for something else. A trophy, for example, is of little value to anyone except the person who won it; it is a *symbol* of his success in an endeavor.

What values do the following objects represent? To what extent are they practical values, and to what extent symbolic?

an acre of farm land
a diamond engagement ring
a stamp collection
a Ford Mustang

writing assignment

1. Choose your most valued possession. (This must be a material object, not a quality.)
2. Write a full paragraph about how much this possession means to you, giving many specific instances. Let yourself go in expressing your pride in it.
3. Now — and this won't be easy — write a paragraph of equal length expressing an opposite feeling. Pretend that you despise this possession, and give real, convincing reasons, so that your reader will think you are sincere. Do not make up qualities or events that did not happen; just change your attitude toward them. Write as though you were full of resentment.

class writing exercise

Write an essay consisting of four paragraphs about the possession you examined in the previous assignment. It should include:

1. an introductory paragraph telling exactly what the possession is, where it came from, and how you use it
2. a paragraph explaining the advantages of the possession, with as many examples as you can give
3. a paragraph explaining the disadvantages of the possession, with as many examples as you can give
4. a summary paragraph weighing these advantages and disadvantages and evaluating the possession's worth to you.

You are now writing an organized presentation of your experience and your thinking about it. Be sure that your essay has unity — that there is nothing in it that does not contribute to your estimate of the possession's worth.

Give your essay *coherence* as well. *Coherence* is the quality of *sticking together,* the glue that holds the parts of your essay to each other. It is achieved by keeping your reader aware of where you are and what you are doing as you progress from one point to another. If your unity is good, this can be done mostly by means of *transitional expressions* — expressions like *however, because of this, in spite of this, in the first place, in the second place,* and so on. These expressions are like directional signals; they tell your reader where you are changing direction.

Let us say your second paragraph ends and your third begins something like this:

I use my car to go to the swimming pool on hot afternoons and for dragging the main on Saturday night. I enjoy polishing it up in the driveway.

It costs me too much money. The other day I had to buy a new generator, which cost me over thirty dollars.

This sample lacks coherence. It is hard to follow because the relationships among the ideas are not pointed out. Now, let's put in the *transitions* and see how it goes.

I use my car to go to the swimming pool on hot afternoons and for dragging the main on Saturday night. When I am not going anywhere, I enjoy polishing it up in the driveway.

Although it gives me all these pleasures, my car costs me too much money. For example, the other day I had to buy a new generator, which cost me over thirty dollars.

Not only has the passage become clearer, but it has also become smoother and more pleasant to read.

Try to use these devices effectively in your essay.

My Wood

E. M. FORSTER

A few years ago I wrote a book which dealt in part with the difficulties of the English in India. Feeling that they would have had no difficulties in India themselves, the Americans read the book freely. The more they read it the better it made them feel, and a cheque to the author was the result. I bought a wood with the cheque. It is not a large wood – it contains scarcely any trees, and it is intersected, blast it, by a public footpath. Still, it is the first property that I have owned, so it is right that other people should participate in my shame, and should ask themselves, in accents that will vary in horror, this very important question: What is the effect of property upon the character? Don't let's touch economics; the effect of private ownership upon the community as a whole is another question — a more important question, perhaps, but another one. Let's keep to psychology. If you own things, what's their effect on you? What's the effect on me of my wood?

In the first place, it makes me feel heavy. Property does have this effect. Property produces men of weight, and it was a man of weight who failed to get into the Kingdom of Heaven. He was not wicked, that unfortunate millionaire in the parable, he was only stout; he stuck out in front, not to mention behind, and as he wedged himself this way and that in the crystalline entrance and bruised his well-fed flanks, he saw beneath him a comparatively slim camel passing through the eye of a needle and being woven into the robe of God. The Gospels all through couple stoutness and slowness. They point out what is perfectly obvious, yet seldom realized: that if you have a lot of things you cannot move about a lot, that furniture requires dusting, dusters require servants, servants require insurance stamps, and the whole tangle of them makes you think twice before you accept an invitation to dinner or go for a bathe in the Jordan. Sometimes the Gospels proceed further and say with Tolstoy that property is sinful; they approach the difficult ground of asceticism here, where I cannot follow them. But as to the immediate effects of property on people, they just show straightforward logic. It produces men of weight. Men of weight cannot, by definition, move like the lightning from the East unto the West, and the ascent of a fourteen-stone bishop into a pulpit is thus the exact antithesis of the coming of the Son of Man. My wood makes me feel heavy.

In the second place, it makes me feel it ought to be larger.

The other day I heard a twig snap in it. I was annoyed at first, for I thought that someone was blackberrying, and depreciating the value of the undergrowth. On coming nearer, I saw it was not a man who had trodden on the twig and snapped it, but a bird, and I felt pleased. My bird. The bird was not equally pleased. Ignoring the relation between us, it took fright as soon as it saw the shape of my face, and flew straight over the boundary hedge into a field, the property of Mrs. Henessy, where it sat down with a loud squawk. It had become Mrs. Henessy's bird. Something seemed grossly amiss here, something that would not have occurred had the wood been larger. I could not afford to buy Mrs. Henessy out, I dared not murder her, and limitations of this sort beset me on every side. Ahab did not want that vineyard — he only needed it to round off his property, preparatory to plotting a new curve — and all the land around my wood has become necessary to me in order to round off the wood. A boundary protects. But — poor little thing — the boundary ought in its turn to be protected. Noises on the edge of it. Children throw stones. A little more, and then a little more, until we reach the sea. Happy Canute! Happier Alexander! And after all, why should even the world be the limit of possession? A rocket containing a Union Jack, will, it is hoped, be shortly fired at the moon. Mars. Sirius. Beyond which . . . But these immensities ended by saddening me. I could not suppose that my wood was the destined nucleus of universal dominion – it is so very small and contains no mineral wealth beyond the blackberries. Nor was I comforted when Mrs. Henessy's bird took alarm for the second time and flew clean away from us all, under the belief that it belonged to itself.

In the third place, property makes its owner feel that he ought to do something to it. Yet he isn't sure what. A restlessness comes over him, a vague sense that he has a personality to express – the same sense which, without any vagueness, leads the artist to an act of creation. Sometimes I think I will cut down such trees as remain in the wood, at other times I want to fill up the gaps between them with new trees. Both impulses are pretentious and empty. They are not honest movements towards money-making or beauty. They spring from a foolish desire to express myself and from an inability to enjoy what I have got. Creation, property, enjoyment form a sinister trinity in the human mind. Creation and enjoyment are both very, very good, yet they are often unattainable without a material basis, and at such moments property pushes itself in as a substitute, saying, "Accept me instead – I'm good enough for all three." It is not enough. It is, as Shakespeare said of lust, "The expense of spirit in a waste of shame": it is "Before, a joy proposed; behind, a dream." Yet we don't know how to shun it. It is forced on us by our economic system as the alternative to starvation. It is also forced on us by an internal defect in the soul, by the feeling that in property may lie the germs of self-development and of exquisite or heroic deeds. Our life on earth is, and ought to be, material and carnal. But we have not yet learned to manage our materialism and carnality properly; they are still entangled with the desire for ownership, where (in the words of Dante) "Possession is one with loss."

And this brings us to our fourth and final point: the blackberries.

Blackberries are not plentiful in this meagre grove, but they are easily seen from the public footpath which traverses it, and all too easily gathered. Foxgloves, too – people will pull up the foxgloves, and ladies of an educational tendency even grub for toadstools to show them on the Monday in class. Other ladies, less educated, roll down the bracken in the arms of their gentlemen friends. There is paper, there are tins. Pray, does my wood belong to me or doesn't it? And, if it does, should I not own it best by allowing no one else to walk there? There is a wood near Lyme Regis, also cursed by a public footpath, where the owner has not hesitated on this point. He had built high stone walls each side of the path, and has spanned it by bridges, so that the public circulate like termites while he gorges on the blackberries unseen. He really does own his wood, this able chap. Dives in Hell did pretty well, but the gulf dividing him from

Lazarus could be traversed by vision, and nothing traverses it here. And perhaps I shall come to this in time. I shall wall in and fence out until I really taste the sweets of property. Enormously stout, endlessly avaricious, pseudo-creative, intensely selfish, I shall weave upon my forehead the quadruple crown of possession until those nasty Bolshies come and take it off again and thrust me aside into the outer darkness.

---

1. Does Forster buy his "wood" for practical or symbolic reasons? What satisfaction does he expect to get from it?
2. What difficulties come between him and this satisfaction? Are they practical or symbolic?
3. What does the episode of the bird tell him about the nature of property? Who were Canute and Alexander?
4. In his second paragraph Forster refers jokingly to Jesus' saying, "It is easier for a camel to go through the eye of a needle, than for a rich man to enter into the kingdom of God." (Matt. 19:24) Does Forster illustrate that this is true in a worldly sense as well? Can property make us less happy in *this* world? How?
5. When Forster says that property "makes you think twice before you accept an invitation to dinner or go for a bathe in the Jordan," what does he mean by "a bathe in the Jordan"?
6. What does Forster believe is the relationship of property to simple enjoyment and creativity?
7. Have you ever had an experience in which something you owned kept you from having fun or being creative?
8. The unity and organization of this essay are obvious: it is divided into four sections on four aspects of ownership. Where has Forster used transitions to make it coherent? Point out some examples.

Salutation

EZRA POUND

O generation of the thoroughly smug
  and thoroughly uncomfortable,
I have seen fishermen picnicking in the sun,
I have seen them with untidy families,
I have seen their smiles full of teeth
  and heard ungainly laughter.
And I am happier than you are,
And they were happier than I am;
And the fish swim in the lake
  and do not even own clothing.

---

1. Who is Pound addressing in the first two lines? Do you think you might be among those he is speaking to?
2. What is smugness? Does it necessarily involve discomfort?
3. Pound says, "I am happier than you are." Do you accept this statement? Do you think he bases it on any real evidence? Can you think of a person who you are sure is less happy than you are? More happy?
4. Why should happy fishermen have untidy families? Is it possible to be tidy and happy at the same time?
5. What does Pound feel about property ownership? What do you think he values most highly?

---

1. What is a money changer? What seems to be the attitude of this money changer toward money? Point out specific evidences to support your answer.
2. How long would you estimate the wife has been married to him? What is your evidence?
3. Was she pretty when she was younger? What has happened to her mouth? Why? To her hands? Why is her neck becoming wrinkled and puffy?
4. What is her attention fixed upon in the picture?
5. Is the artist trying to tell us that money is evil? What *is* he trying to tell us?

PLATE VII

THE MONEY CHANGER AND HIS WIFE: Marinus van Roijmerswaele The Royal Museum of Fine Arts, Copenhagen

Drawing by Chas. Addams; © 1942 The New Yorker Magazine, Inc.

evaluating a person

Nothing so needs reforming as other people's habits. —*Mark Twain*

When you evaluate a piece of property or a situation, you are trying to predict what you can expect from it. Evaluating a person, then, does not mean trying to find out whether he is "better" or "worse" than someone else; it does not imply any moral judgment. It means that you are attempting to gain some insight into the person's thinking and motives in order to estimate what his reactions to certain circumstances might be, especially those circumstances which involve you.

We are inclined to make quick judgments of people on the basis of one or two qualities which we like or dislike and, like Dr. Coles's Jimmie, in Unit 6, close our eyes to the rest. When you dislike someone, can you give a number of good reasons, or is your dislike based on one aspect of his behavior which annoys you? Do you ever question the motives for this behavior? Are his standards different from your own?

class discussion

Think of a person you prefer to avoid because of some quality or habit of his that annoys you. Describe this quality or habit to the class, and then let the class suggest possible interpretations of his behavior. What does he mean by it? What are the motives behind it?

writing assignment

1. Choose the person you have the least liking for of all those around you.
2. Write a full paragraph, giving as many concrete examples as you can of qualities that make you dislike this person. Exaggerate a little if you wish.
3. Write a second paragraph in which you suggest possible motives for each of these qualities. If *you* were that way, *why* would you be?
4. Now, write a third paragraph about all the good qualities and actions of the same person. Don't make them up, but *find* them. Write about the person as though you were very fond of him. This may be difficult, but give it a good try.

sketching assignment

Examine *Heilige Nacht* by George Grosz at the end of this unit. The picture, of course, is *satiric*: the artist is exaggerating the weaknesses and bad qualities of a middle-class German family.

Ignoring for the moment the satiric aspect of the picture, but using the evidence in it, draw a quick sketch in words of this family enjoying Christmas, stressing any inferences you can make concerning their *good* qualities, or any resemblances you can find between them and your own family.

class writing exercise

Following the same organization you used for the class essay on a possession in Unit 7, write an essay on the good and bad qualities of the person you examined for the writing assignment in this unit. Again, keep in mind unity and coherence.

The Witness

KATHERINE ANNE PORTER

Uncle Jimbilly was so old and had spent so many years bowed over things, putting them together and taking them apart, making them over and making them do, he was bent almost double. His hands were closed and stiff from gripping objects tightly, while he worked at them, and they could not open altogether even if a child took the thick black fingers and tried to turn them back. He hobbled on a stick; his purplish skull showed through patches in his wool, which had turned greenish gray and looked as if the moths had got at it.

He mended harness and put half soles on the other Negroes' shoes, he built fences and chicken coops and barn doors; he stretched wires and put in new window panes and fixed sagging hinges and patched up roofs; he repaired carriage tops and cranky plows. Also he had a gift for carving miniature tombstones out of blocks of wood; give him almost any kind of piece of wood and he could turn out a tombstone, shaped very like the real ones, with carving, and a name and date on it if they were needed. They were often needed, for some small beast or bird was always dying and having to be buried with proper ceremonies: the cart draped as a hearse, a shoe-box coffin with a pall over it, a profuse floral outlay, and, of course, a tombstone. As he worked, turning the long blade of his bowie knife deftly in circles to cut a flower, whittling and smoothing the back and sides, stopping now and then to hold it at arm's length and examine it with one eye closed, Uncle Jimbilly would talk in a low, broken, abstracted murmur, as if to himself; but he was really saying something he meant one to hear. Sometimes it would be an incomprehensible ghost story; listen ever so carefully, at the end it was impossible to decide whether Uncle Jimbilly himself had seen the ghost, whether it was a real ghost at all, or only another man dressed like one; and he dwelt much on the horrors of slave times.

"Dey used to take 'em out and tie 'em down and whup 'em," he muttered, "wid gret big leather strops inch thick long as yo' ahm, wid round holes bored in 'em so's every time dey hit 'em de hide and de meat done come off dey bones in little round chunks. And wen dey had whupped 'em wid de strop till dey backs was all raw and bloody, dey spread dry cawnshucks on dey backs and set 'em afire and pahched 'em, and den dey poured vinega all ovah 'em . . . Yassuh. And den, the ve'y

---

nex day dey'd got to git back to work in the fiels or dey'd do the same thing right ovah agin. Yassah. Dat was it. If dey didn't git back to work dey got it all right ovah agin."

The children — three of them: a serious, prissy older girl of ten, a thoughtful sad looking boy of eight, and a quick flighty little girl of six — sat disposed around Uncle Jimbilly and listened with faint tinglings of embarrassment. They knew, of course, that once upon a time Negroes had been slaves; but they had all been freed long ago and were now only servants. It was hard to realize that Uncle Jimbilly had been born in slavery, as the Negroes were always saying. The children thought that Uncle Jimbilly had got over his slavery very well. Since they had known him, he had never done a single thing that anyone told him to do. He did his work just as he pleased and when he pleased. If you wanted a tombstone, you had to be very careful about the way you asked for it. Nothing could have been more impersonal and faraway than his tone and manner of talking about slavery, but they wriggled a little and felt guilty. Paul would have changed the subject, but Miranda, the little quick one, wanted to know the worst. "Did they act like that to you, Uncle Jimbilly?" she asked.

"No, *mam,*" said Uncle Jimbilly. "Now whut name you want on dis one? Dey nevah did. Dey done 'em dat way in the rice swamps. I always worked right here close to the house or in town with Miss Sophia. Down in the swamps . . ."

"Didn't they ever die, Uncle Jimbilly?" asked Paul.

"Cose dey died," said Uncle Jimbilly, "cose dey died — dey died," he went on, pursing his mouth gloomily, "by de thousands and tens upon thousands."

"Can you carve 'Safe in Heaven' on that, Uncle Jimbilly?" asked Maria in her pleasant, mincing voice.

"To put over a tame jackrabbit, Missy?" asked Uncle Jimbilly indignantly. He was very religious. "A heathen like dat? No, *mam.* In de swamps dey used to stake 'em out all day and all night, and all day and all night and all day wid dey hans and feet tied so dey couldn't scretch and let de muskeeters eat 'em alive. De muskeeters 'ud bite 'em tell dey was all swole up like a balloon all over, and you could heah 'em howlin and prayin all ovah the swamp. Yassuh. Dat was it. And nary a drop of watah noh a moufful of braid . . . Yassuh, dat's it. Lawd, dey done it. Hosanna! Now take dis yere tombstone and don' bother me no more . . . or I'll . . ."

Uncle Jimbilly was apt to be suddenly annoyed and you never knew why. He was easily put out about things, but his threats were always so exorbitant that not even the most credulous child could be terrified by them. He was always going to do something quite horrible to somebody and then he was going to dispose of the remains in a revolting manner. He was going to skin somebody alive and nail the hide on the barn door, or he was just getting ready to cut off somebody's ears with a hatchet and pin them on Bongo, the crop-eared brindle dog. He was often all prepared in his mind to pull somebody's teeth and make a set of false teeth for Ole Man Ronk . . . Ole Man Ronk was a tramp who had been living all summer in the little cabin behind the smokehouse. He got his rations along with the Negroes and sat all day mumbling his naked gums. He had skimpy black whiskers which appeared to be set in wax, and angry red eyelids. He took morphine, it was said; but what morphine might be, or how he took it, or why, no one seemed to know . . . Nothing could have been more unpleasant than the notion that one's teeth might be given to Ole Man Ronk.

The reason why Uncle Jimbilly never did any of these things he threatened was, he said, because he never could get round to them. He always had so much other work on hand he never seemed to get caught up on it. But some day, somebody was going to get a mighty big surprise, and meanwhile everybody had better look out.

---

1. Joel Chandler Harris' Uncle Remus stories, mostly about Brer Rabbit and his clever triumphs over powerful but gullible enemies such as Brer Fox, are told by a benevolent old white-haired Negro who likes to have the children gather about his knees and listen. Uncle Jimbilly is a *parody* of Uncle Remus – that is, a parallel created for quite different purposes: he makes tombstones for rabbits. Why does he like to make tombstones?
2. How do the children (and presumably their parents) regard Uncle Jimbilly? Do they understand what he is really like?
3. Uncle Jimbilly "was very religious." What form does his religion take? What satisfaction does he get from it?
4. Who does Ole Man Ronk stand for in Uncle Jimbilly's mind? When he threatens to give the children's teeth to him, what connection does this have with the sufferings of the slaves?
5. In telling about Uncle Jimbilly, what qualities has the author emphasized? Point out expressions which show her emphasis.
6. If Uncle Jimbilly and the children both achieved greater contact with each other, what might they find out about each other?

Innocence

THOM GUNN

He ran the course and as he ran he grew,
And smelt his fragrance in the field. Already,
Running he knew the most he ever knew,
The egotism of a healthy body.

Ran into manhood, ignorant of the past:
Culture of guilt and guilt's vague heritage,
Self-pity and the soul; what he possessed
Was rich, potential, like the bud's tipped rage.

The Corps developed, it was plain to see,
Courage, endurance, loyalty and skill
To a morale firm as morality,
Hardening him to an instrument, until

The finitude of virtues that were there
Bodied within the swarthy uniform
A compact innocence, child-like and clear,
No doubt could penetrate, no act could harm.

When he stood near the Russian partisan
Being burned alive, he therefore could behold
The ribs wear gently through the darkening skin
And sicken only at the Northern cold,

Could watch the fat burn with a violet flame
And feel disgusted only at the smell,
And judge that all pain finishes the same
As melting quietly by his boots it fell.

---

1. What is a synonym for *innocence?*
2. Is innocence usually considered a desirable quality? Why? What does it have to do with contact?
3. In what ways is the boy who is the subject of the poem innocent? What is he innocent of?
4. Because of his good traits most people would consider the boy a desirable kind of person. Under what circumstances might they discover they were wrong?
5. The poet says "No doubt could penetrate, no act could harm" his innocence. What does he mean?
6. After watching the torture of the partisan, is the boy still innocent? Were the leaders of Nazi Germany innocent, if we accept Thom Gunn's definition of the word?
7. What is Gunn's evaluation of the boy? How does it differ from most people's?

---

1. In what ways are the members of this family "innocent"? Are they "innocent" in Thom Gunn's sense of the word?
2. Imagine yourself knocking at this family's door during this scene. How would you be received? What conditions might affect your reception?
3. The boy who is the subject of "Innocence" belongs to a large "in group" called The Corps, and to some extent to a larger one, his nation; for him, there are no holds barred when he is dealing with a member of another group, such as the partisan. What "in group" do these people in *Heilige Nacht* belong to? What groups do you think they might feel justified in dealing ruthlessly with?
4. George Grosz has not made a point of showing the good qualities of these people; nevertheless, some are evident. What are they?
5. What parts of their environment do you feel these people have good contact with? What parts do they have incomplete contact with?

PLATE VIII

HEILIGE NACHT: George Grosz   Used with the permission of the Estate of George Grosz, Princeton, New Jersey

Drawing by O. Soglow; © 1964 The New Yorker Magazine, Inc.

9

identifying with a person

No man can justly censure or condemn another, because indeed no man truly knows another. —*Sir Thomas Browne*

In Units 6 and 8 you observed and evaluated a person, and in several of the other units you have been examining your own attitudes. Since people are basically alike in many ways, you can now consciously attempt to apply what you know about yourself to understanding another person. No matter how different from you a person may seem, he, like you, is greatly influenced by his perception of the environment, his emotional attitudes, the beliefs he has been taught, and the limitations of his awareness. Perhaps the most significant of all acts of perception is identifying with another person, feeling what it is like to *be* him – "putting yourself in his shoes."

class exercise

It is not hard to feel sorry for the man pictured in Goya's *The Prisoner* (at the end of this unit), but feeling sorry for him is not the same thing as identifying with him. Try to put yourself in his place. Using the pronoun *I*, show how you feel. What do you wish for most? What is your sense of time like? How do you feel physically? What things do you remember? What are your feelings toward your captors? If you were freed now, what would it mean to you? Would you be a better man? Discuss any other feelings or thoughts you have.

writing assignment

1. Return to the person you used for the previous writing assignment, the person you like least among those around you. Write a full account — several pages — of ten or fifteen minutes in the life of that person *as though you were he.*

   Look for clues in the person's speech, actions, dress, and appearance. What does he talk about most? This may be a clue to the obsessions that run through his mind, like the ones you explored in your own mind in Unit 4. How does he move about? What does he do with his hands? His eyes? His mouth? Does he dress to impress others? If so, what impression does he seem to be trying to make? What does he do with his hair? What kind of facial expressions does he confront others with? Most importantly, as you answer each question, try to imagine, "What would *my* motive be if I did that?"
2. Use *I* throughout, but do not insert *your* personality in place of *his;* try to figure out what *his* thoughts and feelings are from his speech and actions.
3. Focus especially on the thoughts of the person as he appears in the situation in which you usually see him. What does he think about the people he is in contact with, including yourself? How does he justify his attitudes to himself? Get inside his skin.

class writing exercise

Returning to *The Prisoner* at the end of this unit, identify with the *artist.* Write an essay of three or four unified, coherent paragraphs on the subject of imprisonment; in other words, try to express in words what you have tried to express in your picture. Theorize about what you think imprisonment accomplishes and does not accomplish, in terms of both the prisoner and his captors, and give imaginary specific examples suggested by the picture.

Sonny's Blues

JAMES BALDWIN

I read about it in the paper, in the subway, on my way to work. I read it, and I couldn't believe it, and I read it again. Then perhaps I just stared at it, at the newsprint spelling out his name, spelling out the story. I stared at it in the swinging lights of the subway car, and in the faces and bodies of the people, and in my own face, trapped in the darkness which roared outside.

It was not to be believed and I kept telling myself that, as I walked from the subway station to the high school. And at the same time I couldn't doubt it. I was scared, scared for Sonny. He became real to me again. A great block of ice got settled in my belly and kept melting there slowly all day long, while I taught my classes algebra. It was a special kind of ice. It kept melting, sending trickles of ice water all up and down my veins, but it never got less. Sometimes it hardened and seemed to expand until I felt my guts were going to come spilling out or that I was going to choke or scream. This would always be at a moment when I was remembering some specific thing Sonny had once said or done.

When he was about as old as the boys in my classes his face had been bright and open, there was a lot of copper in it; and he'd had wonderfully direct brown eyes, and great gentleness and privacy. I wondered what he looked like now. He had been picked up, the evening before, in a raid on an apartment downtown, for peddling and using heroin.

I couldn't believe it: but what I mean by that is that I couldn't find any room for it anywhere inside me. I had kept it outside me for a long time. I hadn't wanted to know. I had had suspicions, but I didn't name them, I kept putting them away. I told myself that Sonny was wild, but he wasn't crazy. And he'd always been a good boy, he hadn't ever turned hard or evil or disrespectful, the way kids can, so quick, so quick, especially in Harlem. I didn't want to believe that I'd ever see my brother going down, coming to nothing, all that light in his face gone out, in the condition I'd already seen so many others. Yet it had happened and here I was, talking about algebra to a lot of boys who might, every one of them for all I knew, be popping off needles every time they went to the head. Maybe it did more for them than algebra could.

I was sure that the first time Sonny had ever had horse, he couldn't have been much older than these boys were now. These boys, now, were living as we'd been living then, they were growing up with a rush and

---

their heads bumped abruptly against the low ceiling of their actual possibilities. They were filled with rage. All they really knew were two darknesses, the darkness of their lives, which was now closing in on them, and the darkness of the movies, which had blinded them to that other darkness, and in which they now, vindictively, dreamed, at once more together than they were at any other time, and more alone.

When the last bell rang, the last class ended, I let out my breath. It seemed I'd been holding it for all that time. My clothes were wet — I may have looked as though I'd been sitting in a steam bath, all dressed up, all afternoon. I sat alone in the classroom a long time. I listened to the boys outside, downstairs, shouting and cursing and laughing. Their laughter struck me for perhaps the first time. It was not the joyous laughter which — God knows why — one associates with children. It was mocking and insular, its intent was to denigrate. It was disenchanted, and in this, also, lay the authority of their curses. Perhaps I was listening to them because I was thinking about my brother and in them I heard my brother. And myself.

One boy was whistling a tune, at once very complicated and very simple, it seemed to be pouring out of him as though he were a bird, and it sounded very cool and moving through all that harsh, bright air, only just holding its own through all those other sounds.

I stood up and walked over to the window and looked down into the courtyard. It was the beginning of the spring and the sap was rising in the boys. A teacher passed through them every now and again, quickly, as though he or she couldn't wait to get out of that courtyard, to get those boys out of their sight and off their minds. I started collecting my stuff. I thought I'd better get home and talk to Isabel.

The courtyard was almost deserted by the time I got downstairs. I saw this boy standing in the shadow of a doorway, looking just like Sonny. I almost called his name. Then I saw that it wasn't Sonny, but somebody we used to know, a boy from around our block. He'd been Sonny's friend. He'd never been mine, having been too young for me, and, anyway, I'd never liked him. And now, even though he was a grown-up man, he still hung around that block, still spent hours on the street corners, was always high and raggy. I used to run into him from time to time and he'd often work around to asking me for a quarter or fifty cents. He always had some real good excuse, too, and I always gave it to him, I don't know why.

But now, abruptly, I hated him. I couldn't stand the way he looked at me, partly like a dog, partly like a cunning child. I wanted to ask him what the hell he was doing in the school courtyard.

He sort of shuffled over to me, and he said, "I see you got the papers. So you already know about it."

"You mean about Sonny? Yes, I already know about it. How come they didn't get you?"

He grinned. It made him repulsive and it also brought to mind what he'd looked like as a kid. "I wasn't there. I stay away from them people."

"Good for you." I offered him a cigarette and I watched him through the smoke. "You come all the way down here just to tell me about Sonny?"

"That's right." He was sort of shaking his head and his eyes looked strange, as though they were about to cross. The bright sun deadened his damp dark brown skin and it made his eyes look yellow and showed up the dirt in his kinked hair. He smelled funky. I moved a little away from him and I said, "Well, thanks. But I already know about it and I got to get home."

"I'll walk you a little ways," he said. We started walking. There were a couple of kids still loitering in the courtyard and one of them said goodnight to me and looked strangely at the boy beside me.

"What're you going to do?" he asked me. "I mean, about Sonny?"

"Look. I haven't seen Sonny for over a year, I'm not sure I'm going to do anything. Anyway, what the hell *can* I do?"

"That's right," he said quickly, "ain't nothing you can do. Can't much help old Sonny no more, I guess."

It was what I was thinking and so it seemed to me he had no right to say it.

"I'm surprised at Sonny, though," he went on – he had a funny way of talking, he looked straight ahead as though he were talking to himself – "I thought Sonny was a smart boy, I thought he was too smart to get hung."

"I guess he thought so too," I said sharply, "and that's how he got hung. And now about you? You're pretty goddamn smart, I bet."

Then he looked directly at me, just for a minute. "I ain't smart," he said. "If I was smart, I'd have reached for a pistol a long time ago."

"Look. Don't tell *me* your sad story, if it was up to me, I'd give you one." Then I felt guilty – guilty, probably, for never having supposed that the poor bastard *had* a story of his own, much less a sad one, and I asked, quickly, "What's going to happen to him now?"

He didn't answer this. He was off by himself some place. "Funny thing," he said, and from his tone we might have been discussing the quickest way to get to Brooklyn, "when I saw the papers this morning, the first thing I asked myself was if I had anything to do with it. I felt sort of responsible."

I began to listen more carefully. The subway station was on the corner, just before us, and I stopped. He stopped, too. We were in front of a bar and he ducked slightly, peering in, but whoever he was looking for didn't seem to be there. The juke box was blasting away with something black and bouncy and I half watched the barmaid as she danced her way from the juke box to her place behind the bar. And I watched her face as she laughingly responded to something someone said to her, still keeping time to the music. When she smiled one saw the little girl, one sensed the doomed, still-struggling woman beneath the battered face of the semi-whore.

"I never *give* Sonny nothing," the boy said finally, "but a long time ago I come to school high and Sonny asked me how it felt." He paused, I couldn't bear to watch him, I watched the barmaid, and I listened to the music which seemed to be causing the pavement to shake. "I told him it felt great." The music stopped, the barmaid paused and watched the juke box until the music began again. "It did."

All this was carrying me some place I didn't want to go. I certainly didn't want to know how it felt. It filled everything the people, the houses, the music, the dark, quicksilver barmaid, with menace; and this menace was their reality.

"What's going to happen to him now?" I asked again.

"They'll send him away some place and they'll try to cure him." He shook his head. "Maybe he'll even think he's kicked the habit. Then they'll let him loose" — he gestured, throwing his cigarette into the gutter. "That's all."

"What do you mean, that's *all?*"

But I knew what he meant.

"I *mean,* that's *all.*" He turned his head and looked at me, pulling down the corners of his mouth. "Don't you know what I mean?" he asked, softly.

"How the hell *would* I know what you mean?" I almost whispered it, I don't know why.

"That's right," he said to the air, "how would *he* know what I mean?" He turned toward me again, patient and calm, and yet I somehow felt him shaking, shaking as though he were going to fall apart. I felt that ice in my guts again, the dread I'd felt all afternoon; and again I watched the barmaid, moving about the bar, washing glasses, and singing. "Listen. They'll let him out and then it'll just start all over again. That's what I mean."

"You mean — they'll let him out. And then he'll just start working his way back in again. You mean he'll never kick the habit. Is that what you mean?"

"That's right," he said, cheerfully. "*You* see what I mean."

"Tell me," I said it last, "why does he want to die? He must want to die, he's killing himself, why does he want to die?"

He looked at me in surprise. He licked his lips. "He don't want to die. He wants to live. Don't nobody want to die, ever."

Then I wanted to ask him – too many things. He could not have answered, or if he had, I could not have borne the answers. I started walking. "Well, I guess it's none of my business."

"It's going to be rough on old Sonny," he said. We reached the subway station. "This is your station?" he asked. I nodded. I took one step down. "Damn!" he said, suddenly. I looked up at him. He grinned again. "Damn it if I didn't leave all my money home. You ain't got a dollar on you, have you? Just for a couple of days, is all."

All at once something inside gave and threatened to come pouring out of me. I didn't hate him any more. I felt that in another moment I'd start crying like a child.

"Sure," I said. "Don't sweat." I looked in my wallet and didn't have a dollar, I only had a five. "Here," I said. "That hold you?"

He didn't look at it – he didn't want to look at it. A terrible, closed look came over his face, as though he were keeping the number on the bill a secret from him and me. "Thanks," he said, and now he was dying to see me go. "Don't worry about Sonny. Maybe I'll write him or something."

"Sure," I said. "You do that. So long."

"Be seeing you," he said. I went on down the steps.

And I didn't write Sonny or send him anything for a long time. When I finally did, it was just after my little girl died, he wrote me back a letter which made me feel like a bastard.

Here's what he said:

Dear brother,

You don't know how much I needed to hear from you. I wanted to write you many a time but I dug how much I must have hurt you and so I didn't write. But now I feel like a man who's been trying to climb up out of some deep, real deep and funky hole and just saw the sun up there, outside. I got to get outside.

I can't tell you much about how I got here. I mean I don't know how to tell you. I guess I was afraid of something or I was trying to escape from something and you know I have never been very strong in the head (smile). I'm glad Mama and Daddy are dead and can't see what's happened to their son and I swear if I'd known what I was doing I would never have hurt you so, you and a lot of other fine people who were nice to me and who believed in me.

I don't want you to think it had anything to do with me being a musician. It's more than that. Or maybe less than that. I can't get anything straight in my head down here and I try not to think about what's going to happen to me when I get outside again. Sometime I think I'm going to flip and *never* get outside and sometime I think I'll come straight back. I tell you one thing, though, I'd rather blow my brains out than go through this again. But that's what they all say, so they tell me. If I tell you when I'm coming to New York and if you could meet me, I sure would appreciate it. Give my love to Isabel and the kids and I was sure sorry to hear about little Gracie. I wish I could be like Mama and say the Lord's will be done, but I don't know it seems to me that trouble is the one thing that never does get stopped and I don't know what good it does to blame it on the Lord. But maybe it does some good if you believe it.

Your brother,
Sonny

Then I kept in constant touch with him and I sent him whatever I could and I went to meet him when he came back to New York. When I saw him many things I thought I had forgotten came flooding back to me. This was because I had begun, finally, to wonder about Sonny, about the life that Sonny lived inside. This life, whatever it was, had made him older and thinner and it had deepened the distant stillness in which he had always moved. He looked very unlike my baby brother. Yet, when he smiled, when we shook hands, the baby brother I'd never known looked out from the depths of his private life, like an animal waiting to be coaxed into the light.

"How you been keeping?" he asked me.

"All right. And you?"

"Just fine." He was smiling all over his face. "It's good to see you again."

"It's good to see you."

The seven years' difference in our ages lay between us like a chasm: I wondered if these years would ever operate between us as a bridge. I was remembering, and it made it hard to catch my breath, that I had been there when he was born; and I had heard the first words he had ever spoken. When he started to walk, he walked from our mother straight to me. I caught him just before he fell when he took the first steps he ever took in this world.

"How's Isabel?"

"Just fine. She's dying to see you."

"And the boys?"

"They're fine, too. They're anxious to see their uncle."

"Oh, come on. You know they don't remember me."

"Are you kidding? Of course they remember you."

He grinned again. We got into a taxi. We had a lot to say to each other, far too much to know how to begin.

As the taxi began to move, I asked, "You still want to go to India?"

He laughed. "You still remember that. Hell, no. This place is Indian enough for me."

"It used to belong to them," I said.

And he laughed again. "They damn sure knew what they were doing when they got rid of it."

Years ago, when he was around fourteen, he'd been all hipped on the idea of going to India. He read books about people sitting on rocks, naked, in all kinds of weather, but mostly bad, naturally, and walking barefoot through hot coals and arriving at wisdom. I used to say that it sounded to me as though they were getting away from wisdom as fast as they could. I think he sort of looked down on me for that.

"Do you mind," he asked, "if we have the driver drive alongside the park? On the west side — I haven't seen the city in so long."

"Of course not," I said. I was afraid that I might sound as though I were humoring him, but I hoped he wouldn't take it that way.

So we drove along, between the green of the park and the stony, lifeless elegance of hotels and apartment buildings, toward the vivid, killing streets of our childhood. These streets hadn't changed, though housing projects jutted up out of them now like rocks in the middle of a boiling sea. Most of the houses in which we had grown up had vanished, as had the stores from which we had stolen, the basements in which we had first tried sex, the rooftops from which we had hurled tin cans and bricks. But houses exactly like the houses of our past yet dominated the landscape, boys exactly like the boys we once had been found themselves smothering in these houses, came down into the streets for light and air and found themselves encircled by disaster. Some escaped the trap, most didn't. Those who got out always left something of themselves behind, as some animals amputate a leg and leave it in the trap. It might be said, perhaps, that I had escaped, after all, I was a school teacher; or that Sonny had, he hadn't lived in Harlem for years. Yet, as the cab moved uptown through streets which seemed, with a rush, to darken with dark people, and as I covertly studied Sonny's face, it came to me that what we both were seeking through our separate cab windows was that part of ourselves which had been left behind. It's always at the hour of trouble and confrontation that the missing member aches.

We hit 110th Street and started rolling up Lenox Avenue. And I'd known this avenue all my life, but it seemed to me again, as it had seemed on the day I'd first heard about Sonny's trouble, filled with a hidden menace which was its very breath of life.

"We almost there," said Sonny.

"Almost." We were both too nervous to say anything more.

We live in a housing project. It hasn't been up long. A few days after it was up it seemed uninhabitably new, now, of course, it's already rundown. It looks like a parody of the good, clean, faceless life — God knows the people who live in it do their best to make it a parody. The beat-looking grass lying around isn't enough to make their lives green, the hedges will never hold out the streets, and they know it. The big windows fool no one, they aren't big enough to make space out of no space. They don't bother with the windows, they watch the TV screen instead. The playground is most popular with the children who don't play at jacks, or skip rope, or roller skate, or swing, and they can be found in it after dark. We moved in partly because it's not too far from where I teach, and partly for the kids; but it's really just like the houses in which Sonny and I grew up. The same things happen, they'll have the same things to remember. The moment Sonny and I started into the house I had the feeling that I was simply bringing him back into the danger he had almost died trying to escape.

Sonny has never been talkative. So I don't know why I was sure he'd be dying to talk to me when supper was over the first night. Everything went fine, the oldest boy remembered him, and the youngest boy liked him, and Sonny had remembered to bring something for each of them; and Isabel, who is really much nicer than I am, more open and giving, had gone to a lot of trouble about dinner and was genuinely glad to see him. And she's always been able to tease Sonny in a way that I haven't. It was nice to see her face so vivid again and to hear her laugh and watch her make Sonny laugh. She wasn't, or, anyway, she didn't seem to be, at all uneasy or embarrassed. She chatted as though there were no subject which had to be avoided and she got Sonny past his first, faint stiffness. And thank God she was there, for I was filled with that icy dread again. Everything I did seemed awkward to me, and everything I said sounded freighted with hidden meaning. I was trying to remember everything I'd heard about dope addiction and I couldn't help watching Sonny for signs. I wasn't doing it out of malice. I was trying to find out something about my brother. I was dying to hear him tell me he was safe.

"Safe!" my father grunted, whenever Mama suggested trying to move to a neighborhood which might be safer for children. "Safe, hell! Ain't no place safe for kids, nor nobody."

He always went on like this, but he wasn't, ever, really as bad as he sounded, not even on weekends, when he got drunk. As a matter of fact, he was always on the lookout for "something a little better," but he died before he found it. He died suddenly, during a drunken weekend in the middle of the war, when Sonny was fifteen. He and Sonny hadn't ever got on too well. And this was partly because Sonny was the apple of his father's eye. It was because he loved Sonny so much and was frightened for him, that he was always fighting with him. It doesn't do any good to fight with Sonny. Sonny just moves back, inside himself, where he can't be reached. But the principal reason that they never hit it off is that they were so much alike. Daddy was big and rough and loud-talking, just the opposite of Sonny, but they both had — the same privacy.

Mama tried to tell me something about this, just after Daddy died. I was home on leave from the army.

This was the last time I ever saw my mother alive. Just the same, this picture gets all mixed up in my mind with pictures I had of her when she was younger. The way I always see her is the way she used to be on a Sunday afternoon, say, when the old folks were talking after the big Sunday dinner. I always see her wearing pale blue. She'd be sitting on the sofa. And my father would be sitting in the easy chair, not far from her. And the living room would be full of church folks and relatives. There they sit, in chairs all around the living room, and the night is creeping up outside, but nobody knows it yet. You can see the darkness growing against the windowpanes and you hear the street noises every now and again, or maybe the jangling beat of a tambourine from one of the churches close by, but it's real quiet in the room. For a moment nobody's talking, but every face looks darkening, like the sky outside. And my mother rocks a little from the waist, and my father's eyes are closed. Everyone is looking at something a child can't see. For a minute they've forgotten the children. Maybe a kid is lying on the rug, half asleep. Maybe somebody's got a kid in his lap and is absent-mindedly stroking the kid's head. Maybe there's a kid, quiet and big-eyed, curled up in a big chair in the corner. The silence, the darkness coming, and the darkness in the faces frighten the child obscurely. He hopes that the hand which strokes his forehead will never stop — will never die. He hopes that there will never come a time when the old folks won't be sitting around the living room, talking about where they've come from, and what they've seen, and what's happened to them and their kinfolk.

But something deep and watchful in the child knows that this is bound to end, is already ending. In a moment someone will get up and turn on the light. Then the old folks will remember the children and they won't talk any more that day. And when light fills the room, the child is filled with darkness. He knows that every time this happens he's moved just a little closer to that darkness outside. The darkness outside is what the old folks have been talking about. It's what they've come from. It's what they endure. The child knows that they won't talk any more because if he knows too much about what's happened to *them,* he'll know too much too soon, about what's going to happen to *him.*

The last time I talked to my mother, I remember I was restless. I wanted to get out and see Isabel. We weren't married then and we had a lot to straighten out between us.

There Mama sat, in black, by the window. She was humming an old church song, *Lord, you brought me from a long ways off.* Sonny was out somewhere. Mama kept watching the streets.

"I don't know," she said, "if I'll ever see you again, after you go off from here. But I hope you'll remember the things I tried to teach you."

"Don't talk like that," I said, and smiled. "You'll be here a long time yet."

She smiled, too, but she said nothing. She was quiet for a long time. And I said, "Mama, don't you worry about nothing. I'll be writing all the time, and you be getting the checks. . . ."

"I want to talk to you about your brother," she said, suddenly. "If anything happens to me he ain't going to have nobody to look out for him."

"Mama," I said, "ain't nothing going to happen to you *or* Sonny. Sonny's all right. He's a good boy and he's got good sense."

"It ain't a question of his being a good boy," Mama said, "nor of his having good sense. It ain't only the bad ones, nor yet the dumb ones that gets sucked under." She stopped, looking at me. "Your Daddy once had a brother," she said, and she smiled in a way that made me feel she was in pain. "You didn't never know that, did you?"

"No," I said, "I never knew that," and I watched her face.

"Oh, yes," she said, "your Daddy had a brother." She looked out of the window again. "I know you never saw your Daddy cry. But *I* did—many a time, through all these years."

I asked her, "What happened to his brother? How come nobody's ever talked about him?"

This was the first time I ever saw my mother look old.

"His brother got killed," she said, "when he was just a little younger than you are now. I knew him. He was a fine boy. He was maybe a little full of the devil, but he didn't mean nobody no harm."

Then she stopped and the room was silent, exactly as it had sometimes been on those Sunday afternoons. Mama kept looking out into the streets.

"He used to have a job in the mill," she said, "and, like all young folks, he just liked to perform on Saturday nights. Saturday nights, him and your father would drift around to different places, go to dances and things like that, or just sit around with people they knew, and your father's brother would sing, he had a fine voice, and play along with himself on his guitar. Well, this particular Saturday night, him and your father was coming home from some place, and they were both a little drunk and there was a moon that night, it was bright like day. Your father's brother was feeling kind of good, and he was whistling to himself, and he had his guitar slung over his shoulder. They was coming down a hill and beneath them was a road that turned off from the highway. Well, your father's brother, being always kind of frisky, decided to run down this hill, and he did, with that guitar banging and clanging behind him, and he ran across the road, and he was making water behind a tree. And your father was sort of amused at him and he was still coming down the hill, kind of slow. Then he heard a car motor and that same minute his brother stepped from behind the tree, into the road, in the moonlight. And he started to cross the road. And your father started to run down the hill, he says he don't know why. This car was full of white men. They was all drunk, and when they seen your father's brother they let out a great whoop and holler and they aimed the car straight at him. They was having fun, they just wanted to scare him, the way they do sometimes, you know. But they was drunk. And I guess the boy, being drunk, too, and scared, kind of lost his head. By the time he jumped it was too late. Your father says he heard his brother scream when the car rolled over him, and he heard the wood of that guitar when it give, and he heard them strings go flying, and he heard them white men shouting, and the car kept on a-going and it ain't stopped till this day. And, time your father got down the hill, his brother weren't nothing but blood and pulp."

Tears were gleaming on my mother's face. There wasn't anything I could say.

"He never mentioned it," she said, "because I never let him mention it before you children. Your Daddy was like a crazy man that night and for many a night thereafter. He says he never in his life seen anything as dark as that road after the lights of that car had gone away. Weren't nothing, weren't nobody on that road, just your Daddy and his brother and that busted guitar. Oh, yes. Your Daddy never did really get right again. Till the day he died he weren't sure but that every white man he saw was the man that killed his brother."

She stopped and took out her handkerchief and dried her eyes and looked at me.

"I ain't telling you all this," she said, "to make you scared or bitter or to make you hate nobody. I'm telling you this because you got a brother. And the world ain't changed."

I guess I didn't want to believe this. I guess she saw this in my face. She turned away from me, toward the window again, searching those streets.

"But I praise my Redeemer," she said at last, "that He called your Daddy home before me. I ain't saying it to throw no flowers at myself, but, I declare, it keeps me from feeling too cast down to know I helped your father get safely through this world. Your father always acted like he was the roughest, strongest man on earth. And everybody took him to be like that. But if he hadn't had *me* there — to see his tears!"

She was crying again. Still, I couldn't move. I said, "Lord, Lord, Mama, I didn't know it was like that."

"Oh, honey," she said, "there's a lot that you don't know. But you are going to find it out." She stood up from the window and came over to me. "You got to hold on to your brother," she said, "and don't let him fall, no matter what it looks like is happening to him and no matter how evil you gets with him. You going to be evil with him many a time. But don't you forget what I told you, you hear?"

"I won't forget," I said. "Don't you worry, I won't forget. I won't let nothing happen to Sonny."

My mother smiled as though she were amused at something she saw in my face. Then, "You may not be able to stop nothing from happening. But you got to let him know you's *there*."

Two days later I was married, and then I was gone. And I had a lot of things on my mind and I pretty well forgot my promise to Mama until I got shipped home on a special furlough for her funeral.

And, after the funeral, with just Sonny and me alone in the empty kitchen, I tried to find out something about him.

"What do you want to do?" I asked him.

"I'm going to be a musician," he said.

For he had graduated, in the time I had been away, from dancing to the juke box to finding out who was playing what, and what they were doing with it, and he had bought himself a set of drums.

"You mean, you want to be a drummer?" I somehow had the feeling that being a drummer might be all right for other people but not for my brother Sonny.

"I don't think," he said, looking at me very gravely, "that I'll ever be a good drummer. But I think I can play a piano."

I frowned. I'd never played the role of the older brother quite so seriously before, had scarcely ever, in fact, *asked* Sonny a damn thing. I sensed myself in the presence of something I didn't really know how to handle, didn't understand. So I made my frown a little deeper as I asked: "What kind of musician do you want to be?"

He grinned. "How many kinds do you think there are?"

"Be *serious,*" I said.

He laughed, throwing his head back, and then looked at me. "I *am* serious."

"Well, then, for Christ's sake, stop kidding around and answer a serious question. I mean, do you want to be a concert pianist, you want to play classical music and all that, or — or what?" Long before I finished he was laughing again. "For Christ's *sake,* Sonny!"

He sobered, but with difficulty. "I'm sorry. But you sound so — *scared!*" and he was off again.

"Well, you may think it's funny now, baby, but it's not going to be so funny when you have to make your living at it, let me tell you *that.*" I was furious because I knew he was laughing at me and I didn't know why.

"No," he said, very sober now, and afraid, perhaps, that he'd hurt me, "I don't want to be a classical pianist. That isn't what interests me. I mean" — he paused, looking hard at me, as though his eyes would help me to understand, and then gestured helplessly, as though perhaps his hand would help — "I mean, I'll have a lot of studying to do, and I'll have to study *everything,* but, I mean, I want to play *with* — jazz musicians." He stopped. "I want to play jazz," he said.

Well, the word had never before sounded as heavy, as real, as it sounded that afternoon in Sonny's mouth. I just looked at him and I was probably frowning a real frown by this time. I simply couldn't see why on earth he'd want to spend his time hanging around nightclubs, clowning around on bandstands, while people pushed each other around a dance floor. It seemed — beneath him, somehow. I had never thought about it before, had never been forced to, but I suppose I had always put jazz musicians in a class with what Daddy called "good-time people."

"Are you *serious?*"

"Hell, *yes,* I'm serious."

He looked more helpless than ever, and annoyed, and deeply hurt.

I suggested, helpfully: "You mean — like Louis Armstrong?"

His face closed as though I'd struck him. "No. I'm not talking about none of that old-time, down home crap."

"Well, look, Sonny, I'm sorry, don't get mad. I just don't altogether get it, that's all. Name somebody — you know, a jazz musician you admire."

"Bird."

"Who?"

"Bird! Charlie Parker! Don't they teach you nothing in the goddamn army?"

I lit a cigarette. I was surprised and then a little amused to discover that I was trembling. "I've been out of touch," I said. "You'll have to be patient with me. Now. Who's this Parker character?"

"He's just one of the greatest jazz musicians alive," said Sonny, sullenly, his hands in his pockets, his back to me. "Maybe *the* greatest," he added, bitterly, "that's probably why *you* never heard of him."

"All right," I said, "I'm ignorant. I'm sorry. I'll go out and buy all the cat's records right away, all right?"

"It don't," said Sonny, with dignity, "make any difference to me. I don't care what you listen to. Don't do me no favors."

I was beginning to realize that I'd never seen him so upset before. With another part of my mind I was thinking that this would probably turn out to be one of those things kids go through and that I shouldn't make it seem important by pushing it too hard. Still, I don't think it would do any harm to ask: "Doesn't all this take a lot of time? Can you make a living at it?"

He turned back to me and half leaned, half sat, on the kitchen table. "Everything takes time," he said, "and – well, yes, sure, I can make a living at it. But what I don't seem to be able to make you understand is that it's the only thing I want to do."

"Well, Sonny," I said, gently, "you know people can't always do exactly what they *want* to do –"

"*No,* I don't know that," said Sonny, surprising me. "I think people *ought* to do what they want to do, what else are they alive for?"

"You getting to be a big boy," I said desperately, "it's time you started thinking about your future."

"I'm thinking about my future," said Sonny, grimly. "I think about it all the time."

I gave up. I decided, if he didn't change his mind, that we could always talk about it later. "In the meantime," I said, "you got to finish school." We had already decided that he'd have to move in with Isabel and her folks. I knew this wasn't the ideal arrangement because Isabel's folks are inclined to be dicty and they hadn't especially wanted Isabel to marry me. But I didn't know what else to do. "And we have to get you fixed up at Isabel's."

There was a long silence. He moved from the kitchen table to the window. "That's a terrible idea. You know it yourself."

"Do you have a *better* idea?"

He just walked up and down the kitchen for a minute. He was as tall as I was. He had started to shave. I suddenly had the feeling that I didn't know him at all.

He stopped at the kitchen table and picked up my cigarettes. Looking at me with a kind of mocking, amused defiance, he put one between his lips. "You mind?"

"You smoking already?"

He lit the cigarette and nodded, watching me through the smoke. "I just wanted to see if I'd have the courage to smoke in front of you." He grinned and blew a great cloud of smoke to the ceiling. "It was easy." He looked at my face. "Come on, now. I bet you was smoking at my age, tell the truth."

I didn't say anything but the truth was on my face, and he laughed. But now there was something very strained in his laugh. "Sure. And I bet that ain't all you was doing."

He was frightening me a little. "Cut the crap," I said. "We already decided that you was going to go and live at Isabel's. Now what's got into you all of a sudden?"

"*You* decided it," he pointed out. "*I* didn't decide nothing." He stopped in front of me, leaning against the stove, arms loosely folded. "Look, brother. I don't want to stay in Harlem no more, I really don't." He was very earnest. He looked at me, then over toward the kitchen window. There was something in his eyes I'd never seen before, some thoughtfulness, some worry all his own. He rubbed the muscle of one arm. "It's time I was getting out of here."

"Where do you want to *go,* Sonny?"

"I want to join the army. Or the navy, I don't care. If I say I'm old enough, they'll believe me."

Then I got mad. It was because I was so scared. "You must be crazy. You goddamn fool, what the hell do you want to go and join the *army* for?"

"I just told you. To get out of Harlem."

"Sonny, you haven't even finished *school.* And if you really want to be a musician, how do you expect to study if you're in the *army?*"

He looked at me, trapped, and in anguish. "There's ways. I might be able to work out some kind of deal. Anyway, I'll have the G.I. Bill when I come out."

"*If* you come out." We stared at each other. "Sonny, please. Be reasonable. I know the setup is far from perfect. But we got to do the best we can."

"I ain't learning nothing in school," he said. "Even when I go." He turned away from me and opened the window and threw his cigarette out into the narrow alley. I watched his back. "At least, I ain't learning nothing you'd want me to learn." He slammed the window so hard I thought the glass would fly out, and turned back to me. "And I'm sick of the stink of these garbage cans!"

"Sonny," I said, "I know how you feel. But if you don't finish school now, you're going to be sorry later that you didn't." I grabbed him by the shoulders. "And you only got another year. It ain't so bad. And I'll come back and I swear I'll help you do *whatever* you want to do. Just try to put up with it till I come back. Will you please do that? For me?"

He didn't answer and he wouldn't look at me.

"Sonny. You hear me?"

He pulled away. "I hear you. But you never hear anything *I* say."

I didn't know what to say to that. He looked out of the window and then back at me. "OK," he said, and sighed. "I'll try."

Then I said, trying to cheer him up a little, "They got a piano at Isabel's. You can practice on it."

And as a matter of fact, it did cheer him up for a minute. "That's right," he said to himself. "I forgot that." His face relaxed a little. But the worry, the thoughtfulness, played on it still, the way shadows play on a face which is staring into the fire.

But I thought I'd never hear the end of that piano. At first, Isabel would write me, saying how nice it was that Sonny was so serious about his music and how, as soon as he came in from school, or wherever he had been when he was supposed to be at school, he went straight to that piano and stayed there until suppertime. And, after supper, he went back to that piano and stayed there until everybody went to bed. He was at the piano all day Saturday and all day Sunday. Then he bought a record player and started playing records. He'd play one record over and over again, all day long sometimes, and he'd improvise along with it on the piano. Or he'd play one section of the record, one chord, one change, one progression, then he'd do it on the piano. Then back to the record. Then back to the piano.

Well, I really don't know how they stood it. Isabel finally confessed that it wasn't like living with a person at all, it was like living with sound. And the sound didn't make any sense to her, didn't make any sense to any of them — naturally. They began, in a way, to be afflicted by this presence that was living in their home. It was as though Sonny were some sort of god, or monster. He moved in an atmosphere which wasn't like theirs at all. They fed him and he ate, he washed himself, he walked in and out of their door; he certainly wasn't nasty or unpleasant or rude, Sonny isn't any of those things; but it was as though he were all wrapped up in some cloud, some fire, some vision all his own; and there wasn't any way to reach him.

At the same time, he wasn't really a man yet, he was still a child, and they had to watch out for him in all kinds of ways. They certainly couldn't throw him out. Neither did they dare to make a great scene about that piano because even they dimly sensed, as I sensed, from so many thousands of miles away, that Sonny was at that piano playing for his life.

But he hadn't been going to school. One day a letter came from the school board and Isabel's mother got it — there had, apparently, been other letters but Sonny had torn them up. This day, when Sonny came in, Isabel's mother showed him the letter and asked where he'd been spending his time. And she finally got it out of him that he'd been down in Greenwich Village, with musicians and other characters, in a white girl's apartment. And this scared her and she started to scream at him and what came up, once she began — though she denies it to this day — was what sacrifices they were making to give Sonny a decent home and how little he appreciated it.

Sonny didn't play the piano that day. By evening, Isabel's mother had calmed down but then there was the old man to deal with, and Isabel herself. Isabel says she did her best to be calm but she broke down and started crying. She says she just watched Sonny's face. She could tell, by watching him, what was happening with him. And what was happening was that they penetrated his cloud, they had reached him. Even if their fingers had been a thousand times more gentle than human fingers ever are, he could hardly help feeling that they had stripped him naked and were spitting on that nakedness. For he also had to see that his presence, that music, which was life or death to him, had been torture for them and that they had endured it, not at all for his sake, but only for mine. And Sonny couldn't take that. He can take it a little better today than he could then but he's still not very good at it and, frankly, I don't know anybody who is.

The silence of the next few days must have been louder than the sound of all the music ever played since time began. One morning, before she went to work, Isabel was in his room for something and she suddenly realized that all of his records were gone. And she knew for certain that he was gone. And he was. He went as far as the navy would carry him. He finally sent me a postcard from some place in Greece and that was the first I knew that Sonny was still alive. I didn't see him any more until we were both back in New York and the war had long been over.

He was a man by then, of course, but I wasn't willing to see it. He came by the house from time to time, but we fought almost every time we met. I didn't like the way he carried himself, loose and dreamlike all the time, and I didn't like his friends, and his music seemed to be merely an excuse for the life he led. It sounded just that weird and disordered.

Then we had a fight, a pretty awful fight, and I didn't see him for months. By and by I looked him up, where he was living, in a furnished room in the Village, and I tried to make it up. But there were lots of other people in the room and Sonny just lay on his bed, and he wouldn't come downstairs with me, and he treated these other people as though they were his family and I weren't. So I got mad and then he got mad, and then I told him that he might just as well be dead as live the way he was living. Then he stood up and he told me not to worry about him any more in life, that he *was* dead as far as I was concerned. Then he pushed me to the door and the other people looked on as though nothing were happening, and he slammed the door behind me. I stood in the hallway, staring at the door. I heard somebody laugh in the room and then the tears came to my eyes. I started down the steps, whistling to keep from crying, I kept whistling to myself, *You going to need me, baby, one of these cold, rainy days.*

I read about Sonny's troubles in the spring. Little Grace died in the fall. She was a beautiful little girl. But she only lived a little over two years. She died of polio and she suffered. She had a slight fever for a couple of days, but it didn't seem like anything and we just kept her in bed. And we would certainly have called the doctor, but the fever dropped, she seemed to be all right. So we thought it had just been a cold. Then, one day, she was up, playing, Isabel was in the kitchen fixing lunch for the two boys when they'd come in from school, and she heard Grace fall down in the living room. When you have a lot of children you don't always start running when one of them falls, unless they start screaming or something. And, this time, Grace was quiet. Yet, Isabel says that when she heard that *thump* and then that silence, something happened in her to make her afraid. And she ran to the living room and there was little Grace on the floor, all twisted up, and the reason she hadn't screamed was that she couldn't get her breath. And when she did scream, it was the worst sound, Isabel says, that she'd ever heard in all her life, and she still hears it sometimes in her dreams. Isabel will sometimes wake me up with a low, moaning, strangled sound and I have to be quick to awaken her and hold her to me and where Isabel is weeping against me seems a mortal wound.

I think I may have written Sonny the very day that little Grace was buried. I was sitting in the living room in the dark, by myself, and I suddenly thought of Sonny. My trouble made his real.

One Saturday afternoon, when Sonny had been living with us, or, anyway, been in our house, for nearly two weeks, I found myself wandering aimlessly about the living room, drinking from a can of beer, and trying to work up the courage to search Sonny's room. He was out, he was usually out whenever I was home, and Isabel had taken the children to see their grandparents. Suddenly I was standing still in front of the living room window, watching Seventh Avenue. The idea of searching Sonny's room made me still. I scarcely dared to admit to myself what I'd be searching for. I didn't know what I'd do if I found it. Or if I didn't.

On the sidewalk across from me, near the entrance to a barbecue joint, some people were holding an old-fashioned revival meeting. The barbecue cook, wearing a dirty white apron, his conked hair reddish and metallic in the pale sun, and a cigarette between his lips, stood in the doorway, watching them. Kids and older people paused in their errands and stood there, along with some older men and a couple of very tough-looking women who watched everything that happened on the avenue, as though they owned it, or were maybe owned by it. Well, they were watching this, too. The revival was being carried on by three sisters in black, and a brother. All they had were their voices and their Bibles and a tambourine. The brother was testifying and while he testified two of the sisters stood together, seeming to say, amen, and the third sister walked around with the tambourine outstretched and a couple of people dropped coins into it. Then the brother's testimony ended and the sister who had been taking up the collection dumped the coins into her palm and transferred them to the pocket of her long black robe. Then she raised both hands, striking the tambourine against the air, and then against one hand, and she started to sing. And the two other sisters and the brother joined in.

It was strange, suddenly, to watch, though I had been seeing these street meetings all my life. So, of course, had everybody else down there. Yet, they paused and watched and listened and I stood still at the window. *"Tis the old ship of Zion,"* they sang, and the sister with the tambourine kept a steady, jangling beat, *"it has rescued many a thousand!"* Not a soul under the sound of their voices was hearing this song for the first time, not one of them had been rescued. Nor had they seen much in the way of rescue work being done around them. Neither did they especially believe in the holiness of the three sisters and the brother, they knew too much about them, knew where they lived, and how. The woman with the tambourine, whose voice dominated the air, whose face was bright with joy, was divided by very little from the woman who stood watching her, a cigarette between her heavy, chapped lips, her hair a cuckoo's nest, her face scarred and swollen from many beatings, and her black eyes glittering like coal. Perhaps they both knew this, which was why, when, as rarely, they addressed each other, they addressed each other as Sister. As the singing filled the air the watching, listening faces underwent a change, the eyes focusing on something within; the music seemed to soothe a poison out of them; and time seemed, nearly, to fall away from the sullen, belligerent, battered faces, as though they were fleeing back to their first condition, while dreaming of their last. The barbecue cook half shook his head and smiled, and dropped his cigarette and disappeared into his joint. A man fumbled in his pockets for change and stood holding it in his hand impatiently, as though he had just remembered a pressing appointment further up the avenue. He looked furious. Then I saw Sonny, standing on the edge of the crowd. He was carrying a wide, flat notebook with a green cover, and it made him look, from where I was standing, almost like a schoolboy. The coppery sun brought out the copper in his skin, he was very faintly smiling, standing very still. Then the singing stopped, the tambourine turned into a collection plate again. The furious man dropped in his coins and vanished, so did a couple of the women, and Sonny dropped some change in the plate, looking directly at the woman with a little smile. He started across the avenue, toward the house. He has a slow, loping walk, something like the way Harlem hipsters walk, only he's imposed on this his own half-beat. I had never really noticed it before.

I stayed at the window, both relieved and apprehensive. As Sonny disappeared from my sight, they began singing again. And they were still singing when his key turned in the lock.

"Hey," he said.

"Hey, yourself. You want some beer?"

"No. Well, maybe." But he came up to the window and stood beside me, looking out. "What a warm voice," he said.

They were singing *If I could only hear my mother pray again!*

"Yes," I said, "and she can sure beat that tambourine."

"But what a terrible song," he said, and laughed. He dropped his notebook on the sofa and disappeared into the kitchen. "Where's Isabel and the kids?"

"I think they went to see their grandparents. You hungry?"

"No." He came back into the living room with his can of beer. "You want to come some place with me tonight?"

I sensed, I don't know how, that I couldn't possibly say no. "Sure. Where?"

He sat down on the sofa and picked up his notebook and started leafing through it. "I'm going to sit in with some fellows in a joint in the Village."

"You mean, you're going to play, tonight?"

"That's right." He took a swallow of his beer and moved back to the window. He gave me a sidelong look. "If you can stand it."

"I'll try," I said.

He smiled to himself and we both watched as the meeting across the way broke up. The three sisters and the brother, heads bowed, were singing *God be with you till we meet again.* The faces around them were very quiet. Then the song ended. The small crowd dispersed. We watched the three women and the lone man walk slowly up the avenue.

"When she was singing before," said Sonny, abruptly, "her voice reminded me for a minute of what heroin feels like sometimes – when it's in your veins. It makes you feel sort of warm and cool at the same time. And distant. And – and sure." He sipped his beer, very deliberately not looking at me. I watched his face. "It makes you feel – in control. Sometimes you've got to have that feeling."

"Do you?" I sat down slowly in the easy chair.

"Sometimes." He went to the sofa and picked up his notebook again. "Some people do."

"In order," I asked, "to play?" And my voice was very ugly, full of contempt and anger.

"Well" – he looked at me with great, troubled eyes, as though, in fact, he hoped his eyes would tell me things he could never otherwise say – "they *think* so. And *if* they think so – !"

"And what do *you* think?" I asked.

He sat on the sofa and put his can of beer on the floor. "I don't know," he said, and I couldn't be sure if he were answering my question or pursuing his thoughts. His face didn't tell me. "It's not so much to *play*. It's to *stand* it, to be able to make it at all. On any level." He frowned and smiled: "In order to keep from shaking to pieces."

"But these friends of yours," I said, "they seem to shake themselves to pieces pretty goddamn fast."

"Maybe." He played with the notebook. And something told me that I should curb my tongue, that Sonny was doing his best to talk, that I should listen. "But of course you only know the ones that've gone to pieces. Some don't – or at least they haven't *yet* and that's just about all *any* of us can say." He paused. "And then there are some who just live, really, in hell, and they know it and they see what's happening and they go right on. I don't know." He sighed, dropped the notebook, folded his arms. "Some guys, you can tell from the way they play, they on something *all* the time. And you can see that, well, it makes something real for them. But of course," he picked up his beer from the floor and sipped it and put the can down again, "they *want* to, too, you've got to see that. Even some of them that say they don't – *some,* not all."

"And what about you?" I asked – I couldn't help it. "What about you? Do *you* want to?"

He stood up and walked to the window and remained silent for a long time. Then he sighed. "Me," he said. Then: "While I was downstairs before, on my way here, listening to that woman sing, it struck me all of a sudden how much suffering she must have had to go through – to sing like that. It's *repulsive* to think you have to suffer that much."

I said: "But there's no way not to suffer – is there, Sonny?"

"I believe not," he said and smiled, "but that's never stopped anyone from trying." He looked at me. "Has it?" I realized, with this mocking look, that there stood between us, forever, beyond the power of time or forgiveness, the fact that I had held silence – so long! – when he had needed human speech to help him. He turned back to the window. "No, there's no way not to suffer. But you try all kinds of ways to keep from drowning in it, to keep on top of it, and to make it seem – well, like *you.* Like you did something, all right, and now you're suffering for it. You know?" I said nothing. "Well you know," he said, impatiently, "why *do* people suffer? Maybe it's better to do something to give it a reason, *any* reason."

"But we just agreed," I said, "that there's no way not to suffer. Isn't it better, then, just to – take it?"

"But nobody just takes it," Sonny cried, "that's what I'm telling you! *Everybody* tries not to. You're just hung up on the *way* some people try – it's not *your* way!"

The hair on my face began to itch, my face felt wet. "That's not true," I said, "that's not true. I don't give a damn what other people do, I don't even care how they suffer. I just care how *you* suffer." And he looked at me. "Please believe me," I said, "I don't want to see you – die – trying not to suffer."

"I won't," he said, flatly, "die trying not to suffer. At least, not any faster than anybody else."

"But there's no need," I said, trying to laugh, "is there? in killing yourself."

I wanted to say more, but I couldn't. I wanted to talk about will power and how life could be – well, beautiful. I wanted to say that it was all within; but was it? or, rather, wasn't that exactly the trouble? And I wanted to promise that I would never fail him again. But it would all have sounded – empty words and lies.

So I made the promise to myself and prayed that I would keep it.

"It's terrible sometimes, inside," he said, "that's what's the trouble. You walk these streets, black and funky and cold, and there's not really a living ass to talk to, and there's nothing shaking, and there's no way of getting it out – that storm inside. You can't talk it and you can't make love with it, and when you finally try to get with it and play it, you realize *nobody's* listening. So *you've* got to listen. You got to find a way to listen."

And then he walked away from the window and sat on the sofa again, as though all the wind had suddenly been knocked out of him. "Sometimes you'll do *anything* to play, even cut your mother's throat." He laughed and looked at me. "Or your brother's." Then he sobered. "Or your own." Then: "Don't worry. I'm all right now and I think I'll *be* all right. But I can't forget – where I've been. I don't mean just the physical place I've been, I mean where I've *been.* And *what* I've been."

"What have you been, Sonny?" I asked.

He smiled – but sat sideways on the sofa, his elbow resting on the back, his fingers playing with his mouth and chin, not looking at me. "I've been something I didn't recognize, didn't know I could be. Didn't know anybody could be." He stopped, looking inward, looking helplessly young, looking old. "I'm not talking about it now because I feel *guilty* or anything like that – maybe it would be better if I did, I don't know. Anyway, I can't really talk about it. Not to you, not to anybody," and now he turned and faced me. "Sometimes, you know, and it was actually when I was most *out* of the world, I felt that I was in it, that I was *with* it, really, and I could play or I didn't really have to *play,* it just came out of me, it was there. And I don't know how I played, thinking about it now, but I know I did awful things, those times, sometimes, to people. Or it wasn't that I *did* anything to them – it was that they weren't real." He picked up the beer can; it was empty; he rolled it between his palms:

"And other times – well, I needed a fix, I needed to find a place to lean, I needed to clear a space to *listen* – and I couldn't find it, and I – went crazy, I did terrible things to *me,* I was terrible *for* me." He began pressing the beer can between his hands, I watched the metal begin to give. It glittered, as he played with it, like a knife, and I was afraid he would cut himself, but I said nothing. "Oh well. I can never tell you. I was all by myself at the bottom of something, stinking and sweating and crying and shaking, and I smelled it, you know? *my* stink, and I thought I'd die if I couldn't get away from it and yet, all the same, I knew that everything I was doing was just locking me in with it. And I didn't know," he paused, still flattening the beer can, "I didn't know, I still *don't* know, something kept telling me that maybe it was good to smell your own stink, but I didn't think that *that* was what I'd been trying to do – and – who can stand it?" and he abruptly dropped the ruined beer can, looking at me with a small, still smile, and then rose, walking to the window as though it were the lodestone rock. I watched his face, he watched the avenue. "I couldn't tell you when Mama died – but the reason I wanted to leave Harlem so bad was to get away from drugs. And then, when I ran away, that's what I was running from – really. When I came back, nothing had changed, *I* hadn't changed, I was just – older." And he stopped, drumming with his fingers on the windowpane. The sun had vanished, soon darkness would fall. I watched his face. "It can come again," he said, almost as though speaking to himself. Then he turned to me. "It can come again," he repeated. "I just want you to know that."

"All right," I said, at last. "So it can come again. All right."

He smiled, but the smile was sorrowful. "I had to try to tell you," he said.

"Yes," I said. "I understand that."

"You're my brother," he said, looking straight at me, and not smiling at all.

"Yes," I repeated, "yes. I understand that."

He turned back to the window, looking out. "All that hatred down there," he said, "all that hatred and misery and love. It's a wonder it doesn't blow the avenue apart."

We went to the only nightclub on a short, dark street, downtown. We squeezed through the narrow, chattering, jam-packed bar to the entrance of the big room, where the bandstand was. And we stood there for a moment, for the lights were very dim in this room and we couldn't see. Then, "Hello, boy," said a voice and an enormous black man, much older than Sonny or myself, erupted out of all that atmospheric lighting and put an arm around Sonny's shoulder. "I been sitting right here," he said, "waiting for you."

He had a big voice, too, and heads in the darkness turned toward us.

Sonny grinned and pulled a little away, and said, "Creole, this is my brother. I told you about him."

Creole shook my hand. "I'm glad to meet you, son," he said, and it was clear that he was glad to meet me *there,* for Sonny's sake. And he smiled, "You got a real musician in *your* family," and he took his arm from Sonny's shoulder and slapped him, lightly, affectionately, with the back of his hand.

"Well. Now I've heard it all," said a voice behind us. This was another musician, and a friend of Sonny's, a coal-black, cheerful-looking man, built close to the ground. He immediately began confiding to me, at the top of his lungs, the most terrible things about Sonny, his teeth gleaming like a lighthouse and his laugh coming up out of him like the beginning of an earthquake. And it turned out that everyone at the bar knew Sonny, or almost everyone; some were musicians, working there, or nearby, or not working, some were simply hangers-on, and some were there to hear Sonny play. I was introduced to all of them and they were all very polite to me. Yet, it was clear that, for them, I was only Sonny's brother. Here, I was in Sonny's world. Or, rather: his kingdom. Here, it was not even a question that his veins bore royal blood.

They were going to play soon and Creole installed me, by myself, at a table in a dark corner. Then I watched them, Creole, and the little black man, and Sonny, and the others, while they horsed around, standing just below the bandstand. The light from the bandstand spilled just a little short of them and, watching them laughing and gesturing and moving about, I had the feeling that they, nevertheless, were being most careful not to step into that circle of light too suddenly: that if they moved into the light too suddenly, without thinking, they would perish in flame. Then, while I watched, one of them, the small, black man, moved into the light and crossed the bandstand and started fooling around with his drums. Then – being funny and being, also, extremely ceremonious – Creole took Sonny by the arm and led him to the piano. A woman's voice called Sonny's name and a few hands started clapping. And Sonny, also being funny and being ceremonious, and so touched, I think, that he could have cried, but neither hiding it nor showing it, riding it like a man, grinned, and put both hands to his heart and bowed from the waist.

Creole then went to the bass fiddle and a lean, very bright-skinned brown man jumped up on the bandstand and picked up his horn. So there they were, and the atmosphere on the bandstand and in the room began to change and tighten. Someone stepped up to the microphone and announced them. Then there were all kinds of murmurs. Some people at the bar shushed others. The waitress ran around, frantically getting in the last orders, guys and chicks got closer to each other, and the lights on the bandstand, on the quartet, turned to a kind of indigo. Then they all looked different there. Creole looked about him for the last time, as though he were making certain that all his chickens were in the coop, and then he – jumped and struck the fiddle. And there they were.

All I know about music is that not many people ever really hear it. And even then, on the rare occasions when something opens within, and the music enters, what we mainly hear, or hear corroborated, are personal, private, vanishing evocations. But the man who creates the music is hearing something else, is dealing with the roar rising from the void and imposing order on it as it hits the air. What is evoked in him, then, is of another order, more terrible because it has no words, and triumphant, too, for that same reason. And his triumph, when he triumphs, is ours. I just watched Sonny's face. His face was troubled, he was working hard, but he wasn't with it. And I had the feeling that, in a way, everyone on the bandstand was waiting for him, both waiting for him and pushing him along. But as I began to watch Creole, I realized that it was Creole who held them all back. He had them on a short rein. Up there, keeping the beat with his whole body, wailing on the fiddle, with his eyes half closed, he was listening to everything, but he was listening to Sonny. He was having a dialogue with Sonny. He wanted Sonny to leave the shoreline and strike out for the deep water. He was Sonny's witness that deep water and drowning were not the same thing – he had been there, and he knew. And he wanted Sonny to know. He was waiting for Sonny to do the things on the keys which would let Creole know that Sonny was in the water.

And, while Creole listened, Sonny moved, deep within, exactly like someone in torment. I had never before thought of how awful the relationship must be between the musician and his instrument. He has to fill it, this instrument, with the breath of life, his own. He has to make it do what he wants it to do. And a piano is just a piano. It's made out of so much wood and wires and little hammers and big ones, and ivory. While there's only so much you can do with it, the only way to find this out is to try; to try and make it do everything.

And Sonny hadn't been near a piano for over a year. And he wasn't on much better terms with his life, not the life that stretched before him now. He and the piano stammered, started one way, got scared, stopped; started another way, panicked, marked time, started again; then seemed to have found a direction, panicked again, got stuck. And the face I saw on Sonny I'd never seen before. Everything had been burned out of it, and, at the same time, things usually hidden were being burned in, by the fire and fury of the battle which was occurring in him up there.

Yet, watching Creole's face as they neared the end of the first set, I had the feeling that something had happened, something I hadn't heard.

Then they finished, there was scattered applause, and then, without an instant's warning, Creole started into something else, it was almost sardonic, it was *Am I Blue*. And, as though he commanded, Sonny began to play. Something began to happen. And Creole let out the reins. The dry, low, black man said something awful on the drums, Creole answered, and the drums talked back. Then the horn insisted, sweet and high, slightly detached perhaps, and Creole listened, commenting now and then, dry, and driving, beautiful and calm and old. Then they all came together again, and Sonny was part of the family again. I could tell this from his face. He seemed to have found, right there beneath his fingers, a damn brand-new piano. It seemed that he couldn't get over it. Then, for awhile, just being happy with Sonny, they seemed to be agreeing with him that brand-new pianos certainly were a gas.

Then Creole stepped forward to remind them that what they were playing was the blues. He hit something in all of them, he hit something in me, myself, and the music tightened and deepened, apprehension began to beat the air. Creole began to tell us what the blues were all about. They were not about anything very new. He and his boys up there were keeping it new, at the risk of ruin, destruction, madness, and death, in order to find new ways to make us listen. For, while the tale of how we suffer, and how we are delighted, and how we may triumph is never new, it always must be heard. There isn't any other tale to tell, it's the only light we've got in all this darkness.

And this tale, according to that face, that body, those strong hands on those strings, has another aspect in every country, and a new depth in every generation. Listen, Creole seemed to be saying, listen. Now these are Sonny's blues. He made the little black man on the drums know it, and the bright, brown man on the horn. Creole wasn't trying any longer to get Sonny in the water. He was wishing him Godspeed. Then he stepped back, very slowly, filling the air with the immense suggestion that Sonny speak for himself.

Then they all gathered around Sonny and Sonny played. Every now and again one of them seemed to say, amen. Sonny's fingers filled the air with life, his life. But that life contained so many others. And Sonny went all the way back, he really began with the spare, flat statement of the opening phrase of the song. Then he began to make it his. It was very beautiful because it wasn't hurried and it was no longer a lament. I seemed to hear with what burning he had made it his, with what burning we had yet to make it ours, how we could cease lamenting. Freedom lurked around us and I understood, at last, that he could help us to be free if we would listen, that he would never be free until we did. Yet, there was no battle in his face now. I heard what he had gone through, and would continue to go through until he came to rest in earth. He had made it his: that long line, of which we knew only Mama and Daddy.

And he was giving it back, as everything must be given back, so that, passing through death, it can live forever. I saw my mother's face again, and felt, for the first time, how the stones of the road she had walked on must have bruised her feet. I saw the moonlit road where my father's brother died. And it brought something else back to me, and carried me past it, I saw my little girl again and felt Isabel's tears again, and I felt my own tears begin to rise. And I was yet aware that this was only a moment, that the world waited outside, as hungry as a tiger, and that trouble stretched above us, longer than the sky.

Then it was over. Creole and Sonny let out their breath, both soaking wet, and grinning. There was a lot of applause and some of it was real. In the dark, the girl came by and I asked her to take drinks to the bandstand. There was a long pause, while they talked up there in the indigo light and after awhile I saw the girl put a Scotch and milk on top of the piano for Sonny. He didn't seem to notice it, but just before they started playing again, he sipped from it and looked toward me, and nodded. Then he put it back on top of the piano. For me, then, as they began to play again, it glowed and shook above my brother's head like the very cup of trembling.

---

1. The narrator of the story "Sonny's Blues" wants to establish contact with his younger brother, but he finds it difficult to do so. Why? Is the fault his, or Sonny's, or both?
2. When the narrator is telling Sonny to stay in school, Sonny says, "I hear you. But you never hear anything *I* say." What things has the narrator failed to hear? Why doesn't he hear them?
3. What are some of the events which finally bring him closer to identifying with Sonny?
4. After telling about what happened to his father's brother, the narrator's mother says, "You may not be able to stop nothing from happening. But you got to let him know you's *there*." What does she mean? What does this have to do with the death of his little daughter?
5. Would the narrator be able to identify more completely with Sonny if he took drugs himself? How can he be of most value to Sonny?
6. Does the author succeed in identifying with the narrator of the story? What are some of the ways in which he helps you to stand in the narrator's shoes?

Mr. Flood's Party

EDWIN ARLINGTON ROBINSON

Old Eben Flood, climbing alone one night
Over the hill between the town below
And the forsaken upland hermitage
That held as much as he should ever know
On earth again of home, paused warily.
The road was his with not a native near;
And Eben, having leisure, said aloud,
For no man else in Tilbury Town to hear:

"Well, Mr. Flood, we have the harvest moon
Again, and we may not have many more;
The bird is on the wing, the poet says,
And you and I have said it here before.
Drink to the bird." He raised up to the light
The jug that he had gone so far to fill,
And answered huskily: "Well, Mr. Flood,
Since you propose it, I believe I will."

Alone, as if enduring to the end
A valiant armor of scarred hopes outworn,
He stood there in the middle of the road
Like Roland's ghost winding a silent horn.
Below him, in the town among the trees,
Where friends of other days had honored him,
A phantom salutation of the dead
Rang thinly till old Eben's eyes were dim.

Then, as a mother lays her sleeping child
Down tenderly, fearing it may awake,
He set the jug down slowly at his feet
With trembling care, knowing that most things break;
And only when assured that on firm earth
It stood, as the uncertain lives of men
Assuredly did not, he paced away,
And with his hand extended paused again:

"Well, Mr. Flood, we have not met like this
In a long time; and many a change has come
To both of us, I fear, since last it was
We had a drop together. Welcome home!"
Convivially returning with himself,
Again he raised the jug up to the light;
And with an acquiescent quaver said:
"Well, Mr. Flood, if you insist, I might.

"Only a very little, Mr. Flood —
For auld lang syne. No more, sir; that will do."
So, for the time, apparently it did,
And Eben evidently thought so too;
For soon amid the silver loneliness
Of night he lifted up his voice and sang,
Secure, with only two moons listening,
Until the whole harmonious landscape rang —

"For auld lang syne." The weary throat gave out,
The last word wavered, and the song was done,
He raised again the jug regretfully
And shook his head, and was again alone.
There was not much that was ahead of him,
And there was nothing in the town below —
Where strangers would have shut the many doors
That many friends had opened long ago.

---

1. Describe, in as much detail as you can, how Eben Flood would look to a person who did not identify with him.
2. What are some of the things Robinson shows us about Eben that we might not know otherwise? Could he help us to identify with Eben even more? How?
3. Like Sonny, Eben is misunderstood by people around him. Are there any other resemblances between them?

4. What parts of his environment has Eben lost contact with? How do you think this has come about? Have his experiences been in any way similar to Sonny's?
5. If you lived in Tilbury Town, what is the best thing you could do in relation to Eben Flood? (Notice that the question is not what you could do *for* him; perhaps he does not want pity or charity.)

---

1. In *The Prisoner,* Goya seems to be identifying with the prisoner rather than simply showing him impersonally. What details help to make you feel the emotions he feels?
2. The prisoner's face is not visible. Why? Do you think identification with him would be easier if you could see his face?
3. What details help you to guess at what kind of a man he was before he was imprisoned?

PLATE IX

THE PRISONER: Francisco Goya

Drawing by Ton Smits in the *Saturday Review*

10

looking at a custom

> The despotism of custom is everywhere the standing hindrance to human advancement. —*John Stuart Mill*

A *custom* is an established practice, usually one handed down to us. Many customs are no more practical than alternate customs might be: driving on the right-hand side of the road seems to have no advantages over driving on the left, as long as we all agree to use one side or the other. Many of the clothes we wear, especially for dress or business, are not very practical, but are modifications of patterns used by our ancestors and thus look right to us because we are used to them.

Many of our customs are so taken for granted that we do not even notice them. Nodding the head to mean "yes" and shaking it for "no" seem so natural to us that a visit to Greece, where the custom is just the opposite, can be quite confusing. (Try shaking your head and saying "yes" at the same time, and you will see how much a custom can become part of you.) Writing from left to right seems the only logical way to do it until we discover that Arabic is written from right to left and Chinese from top to bottom. Perhaps none of these customs is best; it has been suggested that lines reading in alternate directions would be easiest to read, since the eyes could then move smoothly and continuously without jumping back at each line like a typewriter carriage.

Some of our customs may be harmful, inefficient, or wasteful. Many, such as putting debtors in prison, holding slaves, and keeping women out of public life, have been proved so in the past and have been abandoned. One way to intensify your perception of the world around you is to become aware of customs and examine them. Even if you cannot change a custom you find undesirable, you can evaluate its place in your life more accurately when you see that it *is* merely a custom.

class discussion

Choose for discussion a custom of the school you are presently attending, such as going to lectures, having regular class hours, holding classes in rooms full of seats, working for grades, or having final exams. Try to suggest practical alternatives that would better serve the same purpose – that is, learning the knowledge or the skills you need to learn. See if the majority of the class can agree on a suggested improvement.

writing assignment

1. Pick out a custom or a set of customs which you and the people around you practice. Here are a few suggestions:
   - customs of greeting and introducing people
   - customary clothing for formal occasions
   - using chairs for sitting
   - eating certain things at certain times of day
   - dancing
   - living in one-family dwellings
   - weddings
   - funerals
   - attending a formal dinner

   These are only a few of many possibilities.
2. Describe the custom clearly, giving actual examples from your own experience.
3. Define clearly the *purpose* of the custom. What is it meant to accomplish?
4. Suggest and explain the best possible *alternative* custom you can invent to accomplish this same purpose, and describe the advantages it would have.
5. Evaluate the custom and its alternative, deciding whether or not the custom should be changed.

class writing exercise

Recast the above material into a unified, coherent essay of four or five paragraphs.

A & P

JOHN UPDIKE

In walks these three girls in nothing but bathing suits. I'm in the third checkout slot, with my back to the door, so I don't see them until they're over by the bread. The one that caught my eye first was the one in the plaid green two-piece. She was a chunky kid, with a good tan and a sweet broad soft-looking can with those two crescents of white just under it, where the sun never seems to hit, at the top of the backs of her legs. I stood there with my hand on a box of HiHo crackers trying to remember if I rang it up or not. I ring it up again and the customer starts giving me hell. She's one of these cash-register-watchers, a witch about fifty with rouge on her cheekbones and no eyebrows, and I know it made her day to trip me up. She'd been watching cash registers for fifty years and probably never seen a mistake before.

By the time I got her feathers smoothed and her goodies into a bag – she gives me a little snort in passing, if she'd been born at the right time they would have burned her over in Salem – by the time I get her on her way the girls had circled around the bread and were coming back, without a pushcart, back my way along the counters, in the aisle between the checkouts and the Special bins. They didn't even have shoes on. There was this chunky one, with the two-piece – it was bright green and the seams on the bra were still sharp and her belly was still pretty pale so I guessed she just got it (the suit) – there was this one, with one of those chubby berryfaces, the lips all bunched together under her nose, this one, and a tall one, with black hair that hadn't quite frizzed right, and one of these sunburns right across under the eyes, and a chin that was too long – you know, the kind of girl other girls think is very "striking" and "attractive" but never quite makes it, as they very well know, which is why they like her so much – and then the third one, that wasn't quite so tall. She was the queen. She kind of led them, the other two peeking around and making their shoulders round. She didn't look around, not this queen, she just walked straight on slowly, on these long white prima-donna legs. She came down a little hard on her heels, as if she didn't walk in her bare feet that much, putting down her heels and then letting the weight move along to her toes as if she was testing the

---

floor with every step, putting a little deliberate extra action into it. You never know for sure how girls' minds work (do you really think it's a mind in there or just a little buzz like a bee in a glass jar?) but you got the idea she had talked the other two into coming in here with her, and now she was showing them how to do it, walk slow and hold yourself straight.

She had on a kind of dirty-pink — beige maybe, I don't know — bathing suit with a little nubble all over it, and what got me, the straps were down. They were off her shoulders looped loose around the cool tops of her arms, and I guess as a result the suit had slipped a little on her, so all around the top of the cloth there was this shining rim. If it hadn't been there you wouldn't have known there could have been anything whiter than those shoulders. With the straps pushed off, there was nothing between the top of the suit and the top of her head except just *her*, this clean bare plane of the top of her chest down from the shoulder bones like a dented sheet of metal tilted in the light. I mean, it was more than pretty.

She had sort of oaky hair that the sun and salt had bleached, done up in a bun that was unravelling, and a kind of prim face. Walking into the A & P with your straps down, I suppose it's the only kind of face you *can* have. She held her head so high her neck, coming up out of those white shoulders, looked kind of stretched, but I didn't mind. The longer her neck was, the more of her there was.

She must have felt in the corner of her eye me and over my shoulder Stokesie in the second slot watching, but she didn't tip. Not this queen. She kept her eyes moving across the racks, and stopped, and turned so slow it made my stomach rub the inside of my apron, and buzzed to the other two, who kind of huddled against her for relief, and then they all three of them went up the cat-and-dog-food-breakfast-cereal-macaroni-rice-raisins-seasonings-spreads-spaghetti-soft-drinks-crackers-and-cookies aisle. From the third slot I look straight up this aisle to the meat counter, and I watched them all the way. The fat one with the tan sort of fumbled with the cookies, but on second thought she put the package back. The sheep pushing their carts down the aisle — the girls were walking against the usual traffic (not that we have one-way signs or anything) — were pretty hilarious. You could see them, when Queenie's white shoulders dawned on them, kind of jerk, or hop, or hiccup, but their eyes snapped back to their own baskets and on they pushed. I bet you could set off dynamite in an A & P and the people would by and large keep reaching and checking oatmeal off their lists and muttering "Let me see, there was a third thing, began with A, asparagus, no, ah, yes, applesauce!" or whatever it is they do mutter. But there was no doubt, this jiggled them. A few houseslaves in pin curlers even looked around after pushing their carts past to make sure what they had seen was correct.

You know, it's one thing to have a girl in a bathing suit down on the beach, where what with the glare nobody can look at each other much anyway, and another thing in the cool of the A & P, under the fluorescent lights, against all those stacked packages, with her feet paddling along naked over our checkerboard green-and-cream rubber-tile floor.

"Oh Daddy," Stokesie said beside me. "I feel so faint."

"Darling," I said. "Hold me tight." Stokesie's married, with two babies chalked up on his fuselage already, but as far as I can tell that's the only difference. He's twenty-two, and I was nineteen this April.

"Is it done?" he asks, the responsible married man finding his voice. I forgot to say he thinks he's going to be manager some sunny day, maybe in 1990 when it's called the Great Alexandrov and Petrooshki Tea Company or something.

What he meant was, our town is five miles from a beach, with a big summer colony out on the Point, but we're right in the middle of town, and the women generally put on a shirt or shorts or something before they get out of the car into the street. And anyway these are usually women with six children and varicose veins mapping their legs and nobody, including them, could care less. As I say, we're right in the middle of town, and if you stand at our front doors you can see two banks and the Congregational church and the newspaper store and three real-estate offices and about twenty-seven old freeloaders tearing up Central Street because the sewer broke again. It's not as if we're on the Cape; we're north of Boston and there's people in this town haven't seen the ocean for twenty years.

The girls had reached the meat counter and were asking McMahon something. He pointed, they pointed, and they shuffled out of sight behind a pyramid of Diet Delight peaches. All that was left for us to see was old McMahon patting his mouth and looking after them sizing up their joints. Poor kids, I began to feel sorry for them, they couldn't help it.

Now here comes the sad part of the story, at least my family says it's sad, but I don't think it's so sad myself. The store's pretty empty, it being Thursday afternoon, so there was nothing much to do except lean on the register and wait for the girls to show up again. The whole store was like a pinball machine and I didn't know which tunnel they'd come out of. After a while they come around out of the far aisle, around the light bulbs, records at discount of the Caribbean Six or Tony Martin Sings or some such gunk you wonder they waste wax on, sixpacks of candy bars, and plastic toys done up in cellophane that fall apart when a kid looks at them anyway. Around they come, Queenie still leading the way, and holding a little gray jar in her hand. Slots Three through Seven are unmanned and I could see her wondering between Stokes and me, but Stokesie with his usual luck draws an old party in baggy gray pants who stumbles up with four giant cans of pineapple juice (what do these bums *do* with all that pineapple juice? I've often asked myself) so the girls come to me. Queenie puts down the jar and I take it into my fingers icy cold. Kingfish Fancy Herring Snacks in Pure Sour Cream: 49¢. Now her hands are empty, not a ring or a bracelet, bare as God made them, and I wonder where the money's coming from. Still with that prim look she lifts a folded dollar bill out of the hollow at the center of her nubbled pink top. The jar went heavy in my hand. Really, I thought that was so cute.

Then everybody's luck begins to run out. Lengel comes in from haggling with a truck full of cabbages on the lot and is about to scuttle into that door marked MANAGER behind which he hides all day when the girls touch his eye. Lengel's pretty dreary, teaches Sunday school and the rest, but he doesn't miss that much. He comes over and says, "Girls, this isn't the beach."

Queenie blushes, though maybe it's just a brush of sunburn I was noticing for the first time, now that she was so close. "My mother asked me to pick up a jar of herring snacks." He voice kind of startled me, the way voices do when you see the people first, coming out so flat and dumb yet kind of tony, too, the way it ticked over "pick up" and "snacks." All of a sudden I slid right down her voice into her living room. Her father and the other men were standing around in ice-cream coats and bow ties and the women were in sandals picking up herring snacks on toothpicks off a big glass plate and they were all holding drinks the color of water with olives and sprigs of mint in them. When my parents have somebody over they get lemonade and if it's a real racy affair Schlitz in tall glasses with "They'll Do It Every Time" cartoons stencilled on.

"That's all right," Lengel said. "But this isn't the beach." His repeating this struck me as funny, as if it had just occurred to him, and he had been thinking all these years the A & P was a great big sand dune and he was the head lifeguard. He didn't like my smiling — as I say he doesn't miss much — but he concentrates on giving the girls that sad Sunday-school-superintendent stare.

Queenie's blush is no sunburn now, and the plump one in plaid, that I like better from the back — a really sweet can — pipes up, "We weren't doing any shopping. We just came in for the one thing."

"That makes no difference," Lengel tells her, and I could see from the way his eyes went that he hadn't noticed she was wearing a two-piece before. "We want you decently dressed when you come in here."

"We *are* decent," Queenie says suddenly, her lower lip pushing, getting sore now that she remembers her place, a place from which the crowd that runs the A & P must look pretty crummy. Fancy Herring Snacks flashed in her very blue eyes.

"Girls, I don't want to argue with you. After this come in here with your shoulders covered. It's our policy." He turns his back. That's policy for you. Policy is what the kingpins want. What the others want is juvenile delinquency.

All this while, the customers had been showing up with their carts but, you know, sheep, seeing a scene, they had all bunched up on Stokesie, who shook open a paper bag as gently as peeling a peach, not wanting to miss a word. I could feel in the silence everybody getting nervous, most of all Lengel, who asks me, "Sammy, have you rung up their purchase?"

I thought and said "No" but it wasn't about that I was thinking. I go through the punches, 4, 9, GROC, TOT – it's more complicated than you think, and after you do it often enough, it begins to make a little song, that you hear words to, in my case "Hello (*bing*) there, you (*gung*) happy *pee-pul* (*splat*)!" – the *splat* being the drawer flying out. I uncrease the bill, tenderly as you may imagine, it just having come from between the two smoothest scoops of vanilla I had ever known were there, and pass a half and a penny into her narrow pink palm, and nestle the herrings in a bag and twist its neck and hand it over, all the time thinking.

The girls, and who'd blame them, are in a hurry to get out, so I say "I quit" to Lengel quick enough for them to hear, hoping they'll stop and watch me, their unsuspected hero. They keep right on going, into the electric eye; the door flies open and they flicker across the lot to their car, Queenie and Plaid and Big Tall Goony-Goony (not that as raw material she was so bad), leaving me with Lengel and a kink in his eyebrow.

"Did you say something, Sammy?"

"I said I quit."

"I thought you did."

"You didn't have to embarrass them."

"It was they who were embarrassing us."

I started to say something that came out "Fiddle-de-doo." It's a saying of my grandmother's, and I know she would have been pleased.

"I don't think you know what you're saying," Lengel said.

"I know you don't," I said. "But I do." I pull the bow at the back of my apron and start shrugging it off my shoulders. A couple customers that had been heading for my slot begin to knock against each other, like scared pigs in a chute.

Lengel sighs and begins to look very patient and old and gray. He's been a friend of my parents for years. "Sammy, you don't want to do this to your Mom and Dad," he tells me. It's true, I don't. But it seems to me that once you begin a gesture it's fatal not to go through with it. I fold the apron, "Sammy" stitched in red on the pocket, and put it on the counter, and drop the bow tie on top of it. The bow tie is theirs, if you've ever wondered. "You'll feel this for the rest of your life," Lengel says, and I know that's true, too, but remembering how he made that pretty girl blush makes me so scrunchy inside I punch the No Sale tab and the machine whirs "pee-pul" and the drawer splats out. One advantage to this scene taking place in summer, I can follow this up with a clean exit, there's no fumbling around getting your coat and galoshes, I just saunter into the electric eye in my white shirt that my mother ironed the night before, and the door heaves itself open, and outside the sunshine is skating around on the asphalt.

I look around for my girls, but they're gone, of course. There wasn't anybody but some young married screaming with her children about some candy they didn't get by the door of a powder-blue Falcon station wagon. Looking back in the big windows, over the bags of peat moss and aluminum lawn furniture stacked on the pavement, I could see Lengel in my place in the slot, checking the sheep through. His face was dark gray and his back stiff, as if he'd just had an injection of iron, and my stomach kind of fell as I felt how hard the world was going to be to me hereafter.

---

1. In this story, a boy is motivated by his own feelings to examine a custom and make a decision about it. What is the custom? What are the reasons behind it? Are they sound reasons?
2. What does Sammy find he values more than the custom?
3. Why does he refer to the ordinary customers as "sheep"?
4. What does Sammy mean by his last statement, "I felt how hard the world was going to be to me hereafter"? What kind of price must he pay for following his own convictions rather than custom? Do you think he will ultimately be better or worse for it?
5. What details does Updike use to help you identify with Sammy? Do you think he makes conventional people appear less attractive than they really are?
6. Is Sammy's contact with his environment better or poorer than that of the people around him? Is he aware of anything they are not aware of, or vice versa? What?

Tract

WILLIAM CARLOS WILLIAMS

I will teach you my townspeople
how to perform a funeral
for you have it over a troop
of artists —
unless one should scour the world —
you have the ground sense necessary.

See! the hearse leads.
I begin with a design for a hearse.
For Christ's sake not black —
nor white either — and not polished!
Let it be weathered — like a farm wagon —
with gilt wheels (this could be
applied fresh at small expense)
or no wheels at all:
a rough dray to drag over the ground.

Knock the glass out!
My God — glass, my townspeople!
For what purpose? Is it for the dead
to look out or for us to see
how well he is housed or to see
the flowers or the lack of them —
or what?
To keep the rain and snow from him?
He will have a heavier rain soon:
pebbles and dirt and what not.
Let there be no glass —
and no upholstery, phew!
and no little brass rollers
and small easy wheels on the bottom —
my townspeople what are you thinking of?
A rough plain hearse then
with gilt wheels and no top at all.
On this the coffin lies
by its own weight.

No wreaths please —
especially no hot-house flowers.
Some common memento is better,
something he prized and is known by:
his old clothes — a few books perhaps —
God knows what! You realize
how we are about these things
my townspeople —
something will be found — anything
even flowers if he had come to that.
So much for the hearse.

For heaven's sake though see to the driver!
Take off the silk hat! In fact
that's no place at all for him —
up there unceremoniously
dragging our friend out to his own dignity!
Bring him down — bring him down!
Low and inconspicuous! I'd not have him ride
on the wagon at all — damn him —
the undertaker's understrapper!
Let him hold the reins
and walk at the side
and inconspicuously too!

Then briefly as to yourselves:
Walk behind — as they do in France,
seventh class, or if you ride
Hell take curtains! Go with some show
of inconvenience; sit openly —
to the weather as to grief.
Or do you think you can shut grief in?
What —from us? We who have perhaps
nothing to lose? Share with us
share with us — it will be money
in your pockets.
Go now
I think you are ready.

1. What is the purpose of a funeral ceremony?
2. What specific funeral customs does Williams object to? What is his reason in each case? Is it always the same reason?
3. It seems to be an American custom to hide the physical facts of death. Is this a good or bad custom? Why?
4. Would Williams agree that an expensive funeral is a good way to honor the dead? Why do people want expensive funerals? What does the poet mean by "share with us – it will be money in your pockets"?
5. The plain wagon that Williams suggests for a hearse would be impractical in modern cities, where the cemetery is often miles away. Can you suggest a practical alternative which would have the effect he wants?
6. Apparently Williams believes that awareness of death is an important part of our contact with the environment. Do you agree or disagree? What are your reasons?

---

1. What attitude toward the custom of kissing is the artist expressing here? What sort of observer might have this attitude?
2. Brancusi, as we know from other sculptures, is capable of doing very finely finished work. Why do you think he has left this one in such crude form? Does this have to do with what he is trying to say?
3. Do you think Brancusi would like to eliminate the custom of kissing? Can good customs also be funny? Can you think of examples?
4. Is Brancusi trying to identify with his subject? Why, or why not?

PLATE X

THE KISS: Constantin Brancusi 1908, Philadelphia Museum of Art; The Louise and Walter Arensberg Collection

WILL
MARY
CORA
JONES
Thurber

11

examining a goal

One never rises so high as when one does not know where one is going.
—*Oliver Cromwell*

It has been recognized by large industries that the man with a limited goal is of less value to them than the man with a wide range of interests. William J. J. Gordon, in a fascinating little book called *Synectics* (Harper and Row, 1961), describes a method by which men from different fields but all with broad interests join together in "brainstorming" sessions to attack problems of invention and production; they solve these problems with such techniques as pretending to be an object or employing analogies, using materials from fields as diverse as poetry and biology. A number of large companies hire men of varied education and experience to do nothing but think – about anything they wish. These companies have learned that one brilliant idea, conceived by a man with complete freedom to think, can repay their investment many times over.

Many students think of goals in terms of getting a degree, learning a particular skill, and making a good living. These are sensible goals, but it is possible that even these modest goals are best reached by routes other than the direct one of specialization. The most secure person in an unpredictably changing world is likely to be the most adaptable person, the one who has explored his instincts and abilities, who is aware of many aspects of the world around him, and who therefore has many alternatives.

Financial and social success are not the only goals, either. Perhaps they are not really goals at all, but means to an end which can be defined only in terms of your deepest desires. Ask yourself, not once but every day of your life, "What do I really want most? Is it the same thing that I wanted yesterday?" As you continue to explore yourself and your environment, you will find that your view broadens and your goals change.

class discussion

State to the class what one of your goals is. Then let members of the class ask you questions like, "Why?" "What do you mean by that?" "What do you expect to get out of it?" and so on. Try to answer these questions seriously and honestly, without giving up and saying "I don't know" or falling back on generalities like "Everybody wants that." Why do *you* want it?

writing assignment

1. What is your goal at present? Write down a statement of your goal in *specific* terms. What do you want to be doing on the afternoon of September 22, 1990? Don't answer, "I want to be a surgeon," but write a description of the kind of hospital you would like to work in and the kind of surgery you would like to be doing. Make it as specific as your "here and now" assignments.
2. Now, write the question, "Why do I want to be doing this?" and give a *specific* answer.
3. Under this last statement, write the question "Why?" or "What do I mean by that?" and answer it, again in specific terms. Continue this process as long as you possibly can – repeat the cycle at least fifteen or twenty times.
4. Avoid "going around in circles." If you find yourself repeating answers, you have failed to give a "real" and specific answer to one of the questions above. Find the inadequate answer and change it.
5. What do you find, at this stage, to be your ultimate goal? Write it down as your last statement or paragraph.

class writing exercise

Using the final statement from the previous writing assignment as your *thesis*, write an essay of three or four paragraphs, telling *why* this is your goal and *how* you are setting about to reach it.

A *thesis* is to an essay what a *topic sentence* is to a paragraph. Sometimes it is called a *controlling idea,* because it controls the direction and unity of the essay. It is the *generalization* that you are going to support with *specifics* in the rest of the essay. Look back at the sample essay about Ronnie in the Introduction (p. 3). The *thesis* is the first statement: "Getting my eight-year-old brother, Ronnie, ready to go on a trip is always a memorable experience." The rest of the essay is devoted to supporting this generalization.

An essay of the type you are learning to write is constructed like a freight train. The *thesis* is the engine, supplying power and direction and pulling the rest behind it. The cars are the *paragraphs,* each carrying *a topic sentence* and a load of specific sentences; the couplings are *transitions* holding the cars together, and the caboose is the *conclusion,* letting the reader know the essay has come to an end. It is important to remember that the train exists to carry the freight: the essay is a vehicle for getting the meaningful specifics of your experience to the reader in orderly condition, so that he can unload and use them.

A *thesis* can appear at any point in an essay, just as an engine can either pull or push a train. For a while, however, it will be convenient to let your thesis be your first sentence and let the rest follow. This allows you to review your thesis every once in a while to be sure your paragraphs are still following it.

from Invisible Man

RALPH ELLISON

It goes a long way back, some twenty years. All my life I had been looking for something, and everywhere I turned someone tried to tell me what it was. I accepted their answers too, though they were often in contradiction and even self-contradictory. I was naïve. I was looking for myself and asking everyone except myself questions which I, and only I, could answer. It took me a long time and much painful boomeranging of my expectations to achieve a realization everyone else appears to have been born with: That I am nobody but myself. But first I had to discover that I am an invisible man!

And yet I am no freak of nature, nor of history. I was in the cards, other things having been equal (or unequal) eighty-five years ago. I am not ashamed of my grandparents for having been slaves. I am only ashamed of myself for having at one time been ashamed. About eighty-five years ago they were told they were free, united with others of our country in everything pertaining to the common good, and, in everything social, separate like the fingers of the hand. And they believed it. They exulted in it. They stayed in their place, worked hard, and brought up my father to do the same. But my grandfather is the one. He was an odd old guy, my grandfather, and I am told I take after him. It was he who caused the trouble. On his deathbed he called my father to him and said, "Son, after I'm gone I want you to keep up the good fight. I never told you, but our life is a war and I have been a traitor all my born days, a spy in the enemy's country ever since I give up my gun back in the Reconstruction. Live with your head in the lion's mouth. I want you to overcome 'em with yeses, undermine 'em with grins, agree 'em to death and destruction, let 'em swoller you till they vomit or bust wide open." They thought the old man had gone out of his mind. He had been the meekest of men. The younger children were rushed from the room, the shades drawn and the flame of the lamp turned so low that it sputtered on the wick like the old man's breathing. "Learn it to the younguns," he whispered fiercely; then he died.

But my folks were more alarmed over his last words than over his dying. It was as though he had not died at all, his words caused so much anxiety. I was warned emphatically to forget what he had said and, indeed, this is the first time it has been mentioned outside the family circle. It had a tremendous effect upon me, however. I could never be sure of

---

what he meant. Grandfather had been a quiet old man who never made any trouble, yet on his deathbed he had called himself a traitor and a spy, and he had spoken of his meekness as a dangerous activity. It became a constant puzzle which lay unanswered in the back of my mind. And whenever things went well for me I remembered my grandfather and felt guilty and uncomfortable. It was as though I was carrying out his advice in spite of myself. And to make it worse, everyone loved me for it. I was praised by the most lily-white men of the town. I was considered an example of desirable conduct – just as my grandfather had been. And what puzzled me was that the old man had defined it as *treachery*. When I was praised for my conduct I felt a guilt that in some way I was doing something that was really against the wishes of the white folks, that if they had understood they would have desired me to act just the opposite, that I should have been sulky and mean, and that that really would have been what they wanted, even though they were fooled and thought they wanted me to act as I did. It made me afraid that some day they would look upon me as a traitor and I would be lost. Still I was more afraid to act any other way because they didn't like that at all. The old man's words were like a curse. On my graduation day I delivered an oration in which I showed that humility was the secret, indeed, the very essence of progress. (Not that I believed this – how could I, remembering my grandfather? – I only believed that it worked.) It was a great success. Everyone praised me and I was invited to give the speech at a gathering of the town's leading white citizens. It was a triumph for our whole community.

It was in the main ballroom of the leading hotel. When I got there I discovered that it was on the occasion of a smoker, and I was told that since I was to be there anyway I might as well take part in the battle royal to be fought by some of my schoolmates as part of the entertainment. The battle royal came first.

All of the town's big shots were there in their tuxedoes, wolfing down the buffet foods, drinking beer and whiskey and smoking black cigars. It was a large room with a high ceiling. Chairs were arranged in neat rows around three sides of a portable boxing ring. The fourth side was clear, revealing a gleaming space of polished floor. I had some misgivings over the battle royal, by the way. Not from a distaste for fighting but because I didn't care too much for the other fellows who were to take part. They were tough guys who seemed to have no grandfather's curse worrying their minds. No one could mistake their toughness. And besides, I suspected that fighting a battle royal might detract from the dignity of my speech. In those pre-invisible days I visualized myself as a potential Booker T. Washington. But the other fellows didn't care too much for me either, and there were nine of them. I felt superior to them in my way, and I didn't like the manner in which we were all crowded together into the servants' elevator. Nor did they like my being there. In fact, as the warmly lighted floors flashed past the elevator we had words over the fact that I, by taking part in the fight, had knocked one of their friends out of a night's work.

We were led out of the elevator through a rococo hall into an anteroom and told to get into our fighting togs. Each of us was issued a pair of boxing gloves and ushered out into the big mirrored hall, which we entered looking cautiously about us and whispering, lest we might accidentally be heard above the noise of the room. It was foggy with cigar smoke. And already the whiskey was taking effect. I was shocked to see some of the most important men of the town quite tipsy. They were all there — bankers, lawyers, judges, doctors, fire chiefs, teachers, merchants. Even one of the more fashionable pastors. Something we could not see was going on up front. A clarinet was vibrating sensuously and the men were standing up and moving eagerly forward. We were a small tight group, clustered together, our bare upper bodies touching and shining with anticipatory sweat; while up front the big shots were becoming increasingly excited over something we still could not see. Suddenly I heard the school superintendent, who had told me to come, yell, "Bring up the shines, gentlemen! Bring up the little shines!"

We were rushed up to the front of the ballroom, where it smelled even more strongly of tobacco and whiskey. Then we were pushed into place. I almost wet my pants. A sea of faces, some hostile, some amused, ringed around us, and in the center, facing us, stood a magnificent blonde — stark naked. There was dead silence. I felt a blast of cold air chill me. I tried to back away, but they were behind me and around me. Some of the boys stood with lowered heads, trembling. I felt a wave of irrational guilt and fear. My teeth chattered, my skin turned to goose flesh, my knees knocked. Yet I was strongly attracted and looked in spite of myself. Had the price of looking been blindness, I would have looked. The hair was yellow like that of a circus kewpie doll, the face heavily powdered and rouged, as though to form an abstract mask, the eyes hollow and smeared a cool blue, the color of a baboon's butt. I felt a desire to spit upon her as my eyes brushed slowly over her body. Her breasts were firm and round as the domes of East Indian temples, and I stood so close as to see the fine skin texture and beads of pearly perspiration glistening like dew around the pink and erected buds of her nipples. I wanted at one and the same time to run from the room, to sink through the floor, or go to her and cover her from my eyes and the eyes of the others with my body; to feel the soft thighs, to caress her and destroy her, to love her and murder her, to hide from her, and yet to stroke where below the small American flag tattooed upon her belly her thighs formed a capital

V. I had a notion that of all in the room she saw only me with her impersonal eyes.

And then she began to dance, a slow sensuous movement; the smoke of a hundred cigars clinging to her like the thinnest of veils. She seemed like a fair bird-girl girdled in veils calling to me from the angry surface of some gray and threatening sea. I was transported. Then I became aware of the clarinet playing and the big shots yelling at us. Some threatened us if we looked and others if we did not. On my right I saw one boy faint. And now a man grabbed a silver pitcher from a table and stepped close as he dashed ice water upon him and stood him up and forced two of us to support him as his head hung and moans issued from his thick bluish lips. Another boy began to plead to go home. He was the largest of the group, wearing dark red fighting trunks much too small to conceal the erection which projected from him as though in answer to the insinuating low-registered moaning of the clarinet. He tried to hide himself with his boxing gloves.

And all the while the blonde continued dancing, smiling faintly at the big shots who watched her with fascination, and faintly smiling at our fear. I noticed a certain merchant who followed her hungrily, his lips loose and drooling. He was a large man who wore diamond studs in a shirtfront which swelled with the ample paunch underneath, and each time the blonde swayed her undulating hips he ran his hand through the thin hair of his bald head and, with his arms upheld, his posture clumsy like that of an intoxicated panda, wound his belly in a slow and obscene grind. This creature was completely hypnotized. The music had quickened. As the dancer flung herself about with a detached expression on her face, the men began reaching out to touch her. I could see their beefy fingers sink into the soft flesh. Some of the others tried to stop them and she began to move around the floor in graceful circles, as they gave chase, slipping and sliding over the polished floor. It was mad. Chairs went crashing, drinks were spilt, as they ran laughing and howling after her. They caught her just as she reached a door, raised her from the floor, and tossed her as college boys are tossed at a hazing, and above her red, fixed-smiling lips I saw the terror and disgust in her eyes, almost like my own terror and that which I saw in some of the other boys. As I watched, they tossed her twice and her soft breasts seemed to flatten against the air and her legs flung wildly as she spun. Some of the more sober ones helped her to escape. And I started off the floor, heading for the anteroom with the rest of the boys.

Some were still crying and in hysteria. But as we tried to leave we were stopped and ordered to get into the ring. There was nothing to do but what we were told. All ten of us climbed under the ropes and allowed ourselves to be blindfolded with broad bands of white cloth. One of the men seemed to feel a bit sympathetic and tried to cheer us up as we stood with our backs against the ropes. Some of us tried to grin. "See that boy over there?" one of the men said. "I want you to run across at the bell and give it to him right in the belly. If you don't get him, I'm going to get you. I don't like his looks." Each of us was told the same. The blindfolds were put on. Yet even then I had been going over my speech. In my mind each word was as bright as flame. I felt the cloth pressed into place, and frowned so that it would be loosened when I relaxed.

But now I felt a sudden fit of blind terror. I was unused to darkness. It was as though I had suddenly found myself in a dark room filled with poisonous cottonmouths. I could hear the bleary voices yelling insistently for the battle royal to begin.

"Get going in there!"

"Let me at that big nigger!"

I strained to pick up the school superintendent's voice, as though to squeeze some security out of that slightly more familiar sound.

"Let me at those black sonsabitches!" someone yelled.

"No, Jackson, no!" another voice yelled. "Here, somebody, help me hold Jack."

"I want to get at that ginger-colored nigger. Tear him limb from limb," the first voice yelled.

I stood against the ropes trembling. For in those days I was what they called ginger-colored, and he sounded as though he might crunch me between his teeth like a crisp ginger cookie.

Quite a struggle was going on. Chairs were being kicked about and I could hear voices grunting as with a terrific effort. I wanted to see, to see more desperately than ever before. But the blindfold was as tight as a thick skin-puckering scab and when I raised my gloved hands to push the layers of white aside a voice yelled, "Oh, no you don't, black bastard! Leave that alone!"

"Ring the bell before Jackson kills him a coon!" someone boomed in the sudden silence. And I heard the bell clang and the sound of the feet scuffling forward.

A glove smacked against my head. I pivoted, striking out stiffly as someone went past, and felt the jar ripple along the length of my arm to my shoulder. Then it seemed as though all nine of the boys had turned upon me at once. Blows pounded me from all sides while I struck out as best I could. So many blows landed upon me that I wondered if I were not the only blindfolded fighter in the ring, or if the man called Jackson hadn't succeeded in getting me after all.

Blindfolded, I could no longer control my motions. I had no dignity. I stumbled about like a baby or a drunken man. The smoke had become thicker and with each new blow it seemed to sear and further restrict my lungs. My saliva became like hot bitter glue. A glove connected with my head, filling my mouth with warm blood. It was everywhere. I could not tell if the moisture I felt upon my body was sweat or blood. A blow landed hard against the nape of my neck. I felt myself going over, my head hitting the floor. Streaks of blue light filled the black world behind the blindfold. I lay prone, pretending that I was knocked out, but felt myself seized by hands and yanked to my feet. "Get going, black boy! Mix it up!" My arms were like lead, my head smarting from blows. I managed to feel my way to the ropes and held on, trying to catch my breath. A glove landed in my mid-section and I went over again, feeling as though the smoke had become a knife jabbed into my guts. Pushed this way and that by the legs milling around me, I finally pulled erect and discovered that I could see the black, sweat-washed forms weaving in the smoky-blue atmosphere like drunken dancers weaving to the rapid drum-like thuds of blows.

Everyone fought hysterically. It was complete anarchy. Everybody fought everybody else. No group fought together for long. Two, three, four, fought one, then turned to fight each other, were themselves attacked. Blows landed below the belt and in the kidney, with the gloves open as well as closed, and with my eye partly opened now there was not so much terror. I moved carefully, avoiding blows, although not too many to attract attention, fighting from group to group. The boys groped about like blind, cautious crabs crouching to protect their mid-sections, their heads pulled in short against their shoulders, their arms stretched nervously before them, with their fists testing the smoke-filled air like the knobbed feelers of hypersensitive snails. In one corner I glimpsed a boy violently punching the air and heard him scream in pain as he smashed his hand against a ring post. For a second I saw him bent over holding his hand, then going down as a blow caught his unprotected head. I played one group against the other, slipping in and throwing a punch then stepping out of range while pushing the others into the melee to take the blows blindly aimed at me. The smoke was agonizing and there were no rounds, no bells at three minute intervals to relieve our exhaustion. The room spun round me, a swirl of lights, smoke, sweating bodies surrounded by tense white faces. I bled from both nose and mouth, the blood spattering upon my chest.

The men kept yelling, "Slug him, black boy! Knock his guts out!"

"Uppercut him! Kill him! Kill that big boy!"

Taking a fake fall, I saw a boy going down heavily beside me as though we were felled by a single blow, saw a sneaker-clad foot shoot into his groin as the two who had knocked him down stumbled upon him. I rolled out of range, feeling a twinge of nausea.

The harder we fought the more threatening the men became. And yet, I had begun to worry about my speech again. How would it go? Would they recognize my ability? What would they give me?

I was fighting automatically when suddenly I noticed that one after another of the boys was leaving the ring. I was surprised, filled with panic, as though I had been left alone with an unknown danger. Then I understood. The boys had arranged it among themselves. It was the custom for the two men left in the ring to slug it out for the winner's prize. I discovered this too late. When the bell sounded two men in tuxedoes leaped into the ring and removed the blindfold. I found myself facing Tatlock, the biggest of the gang. I felt sick at my stomach. Hardly had the bell stopped ringing in my ears than it clanged again and I saw him moving swiftly toward me. Thinking of nothing else to do I hit him smash on the nose. He kept coming, bringing the rank sharp violence of stale sweat. His face was a black blank of a face, only his eyes alive – with hate of me and aglow with a feverish terror from what had happened to us all. I became anxious. I wanted to deliver my speech and he came at me as though he meant to beat it out of me. I smashed him again and again, taking his blows as they came. Then on a sudden impulse I struck him lightly and as we clinched, I whispered, "Fake like I knocked you out, you can have the prize."

"I'll break your behind," he whispered hoarsely.

"For *them?*"

"For *me,* sonofabitch!"

They were yelling for us to break it up and Tatlock spun me half around with a blow, and as a joggled camera sweeps in a reeling scene, I saw the howling red faces crouching tense beneath the cloud of blue-gray smoke. For a moment the world wavered, unraveled, flowed, then my head cleared and Tatlock bounced before me. That fluttering shadow before my eyes was his jabbing left hand. Then falling forward, my head against his damp shoulder, I whispered,

"I'll make it five dollars more."

"Go to hell!"

But his muscles relaxed a trifle beneath my pressure and I breathed, "Seven?"

"Give it to your ma," he said, ripping me beneath the heart.

And while I still held him I butted him and moved away. I felt myself bombarded with punches. I fought back with hopeless desperation. I wanted to deliver my speech more than anything else in the world, because I felt that only these men could judge truly my ability, and now this stupid clown was ruining my chances. I began fighting carefully now, moving in to punch him and out again with my greater speed. A lucky blow to his chin and I had him going too – until I heard a loud voice yell, "I got my money on the big boy."

Hearing this, I almost dropped my guard. I was confused: Should I try to win against the voice out there? Would not this go against my speech, and was not this a moment for humility, for nonresistance? A blow to my head as I danced about sent my right eye popping like a jack-in-the-box and settled my dilemma. The room went red as I fell. It was a dream fall, my body languid and fastidious as to where to land, until the floor became impatient and smashed up to meet me. A moment later I came to. An hypnotic voice said FIVE emphatically. And I lay there, hazily watching a dark red spot of my own blood shaping itself into a butterfly, glistening and soaking into the soiled gray world of the canvas.

When the voice drawled TEN I was lifted up and dragged to a chair. I sat dazed. My eye pained and swelled with each throb of my pounding heart and I wondered if now I would be allowed to speak. I was wringing wet, my mouth still bleeding. We were grouped along the wall now. The other boys ignored me as they congratulated Tatlock and speculated as to how much they would be paid. One boy whimpered over his smashed hand. Looking up front, I saw attendants in white jackets rolling the portable ring away and placing a small square rug in the vacant space surrounded by chairs. Perhaps, I thought, I will stand on the rug to deliver my speech.

The the M.C. called to us, "Come on up here boys and get your money."

We ran forward to where the men laughed and talked in their chairs, waiting. Everyone seemed friendly now.

"There it is on the rug," the man said. I saw the rug covered with coins of all dimensions and a few crumpled bills. But what excited me, scattered here and there, were the gold pieces.

"Boys, it's all yours," the man said. "You get all you grab."

"That's right, Sambo," a blond man said, winking at me confidentially.

I trembled with excitement, forgetting my pain. I would get the gold and the bills, I thought. I would use both hands. I would throw my body against the boys nearest me to block them from the gold.

"Get down around the rug now," the man commanded, "and don't anyone touch it until I give the signal."

"This ought to be good," I heard.

As told, we got around the square rug on our knees. Slowly the man raised his freckled hand as we followed it upward with our eyes.

I heard, "These niggers look like they're about to pray!"

Then, "Ready," the man said. "Go!"

I lunged for a yellow coin lying on the blue design of the carpet, touching it and sending a surprised shriek to join those rising around me. I tried frantically to remove my hand but could not let go. A hot, violent force tore through my body, shaking me like a wet rat. The rug was electrified. The hair bristled up on my head as I shook myself free. My muscles jumped, my nerves jangled, writhed. But I saw that this was not stopping the other boys. Laughing in fear and embarrassment, some were holding back and scooping up the coins knocked off by the painful contortions of the others. The men roared above us as we struggled.

"Pick it up, goddamnit, pick it up!" someone called like a bass-voiced parrot. "Go on, get it!"

I crawled rapidly around the floor, picking up the coins, trying to avoid the coppers and to get greenbacks and the gold. Ignoring the shock by laughing, as I brushed the coins off quickly, I discovered that I could contain the electricity — a contradiction, but it works. Then the men began to push us onto the rug. Laughing embarrassedly, we struggled out of their hands and kept after the coins. We were all wet and slippery and hard to hold. Suddenly I saw a boy lifted into the air, glistening with sweat like a circus seal, and dropped, his wet back landing flush upon the charged rug, heard him yell and saw him literally dance upon his back, his elbows beating a frenzied tattoo upon the floor, his muscles twitching like the flesh of a horse stung by many flies. When he finally rolled off, his face was gray and no one stopped him when he ran from the floor amid booming laughter.

"Get the money," the M.C. called. "That's good hard American cash!"

And we snatched and grabbed, snatched and grabbed. I was careful not to come too close to the rug now, and when I felt the hot whiskey breath descend upon me like a cloud of foul air I reached out and grabbed the leg of a chair. It was occupied and I held on desperately.

"Leggo, nigger! Leggo!"

The huge face wavered down to mine as he tried to push me free. But my body was slippery and he was too drunk. It was Mr. Colcord, who owned a chain of movie houses and "entertainment palaces." Each time he grabbed me I slipped out of his hands. It became a real struggle. I feared the rug more than I did the drunk, so I held on, surprising myself for a moment by trying to topple *him* upon the rug. It was such an enormous idea that I found myself actually carrying it out. I tried not to be obvious, yet when I grabbed his leg, trying to tumble him out of the chair, he raised up roaring with laughter, and, looking at me with soberness dead in the eye, kicked me viciously in the chest. The chair leg flew out of my hand and I felt myself going and rolled. It was as though I had rolled through a bed of hot coals. It seemed a whole century would pass before I would roll free, a century in which I was seared through the deepest levels of my body to the fearful breath within me and the breath seared and heated to the point of explosion. It'll all be over in a flash, I thought as I rolled clear. It'll all be over in a flash.

But not yet, the men on the other side were waiting, red faces swollen as though from apoplexy as they bent forward in their chairs. Seeing their fingers coming toward me I rolled away as a fumbled football rolls off the receiver's fingertips, back into the coals. That time I luckily sent the rug sliding out of place and heard the coins ringing against the floor and the boys scuffling to pick them up and the M.C. calling, "All right, boys, that's all. Go get dressed and get your money."

I was limp as a dish rag. My back felt as though it had been beaten with wires.

When we had dressed the M.C. came in and gave us each five dollars, except Tatlock, who got ten for being last in the ring. Then he told us to leave. I was not to get a chance to deliver my speech, I thought. I was going out into the dim alley in despair when I was stopped and told to go back. I returned to the ballroom, where the men were pushing back their chairs and gathering in groups to talk.

The M.C. knocked on a table for quiet. "Gentlemen," he said, "we almost forgot an important part of the program. A most serious part, gentlemen. This boy was brought here to deliver a speech which he made at his graduation yesterday . . ."

"Bravo!"

"I'm told that he is the smartest boy we've got out there in Greenwood. I'm told that he knows more big words than a pocket-sized dictionary."

Much applause and laughter.

"So now, gentlemen, I want you to give him your attention."

There was still laughter as I faced them, my mouth dry, my eye throbbing. I began slowly, but evidently my throat was tense, because they began shouting, "Louder! Louder!"

"We of the younger generation extol the wisdom of that great leader and educator," I shouted, "who first spoke these flaming words of wisdom: 'A ship lost at sea for many days suddenly sighted a friendly vessel. From the mast of the unfortunate vessel was seen a signal: "Water, water; we die of thirst!" The answer from the friendly vessel came back: "Cast down your bucket where you are." The captain of the distressed vessel, at last heeding the injunction, cast down his bucket, and it came up full of fresh sparkling water from the mouth of the Amazon River.' And like him I say, and in his words, 'To those of my race who depend upon bettering their condition in a foreign land, or who underestimate the importance of cultivating friendly relations with the Southern white man, who is his next-door neighbor, I would say: "Cast down your bucket where you are" — cast it down in making friends in every manly way of the people of all races by whom we are surrounded . . .' "

I spoke automatically and with such fervor that I did not realize that the men were still talking and laughing until my dry mouth, filling up with blood from the cut, almost strangled me. I coughed, wanting to stop and go to one of the tall brass, sand-filled spittoons to relieve myself, but a few of the men, especially the superintendent, were listening and I was afraid. So I gulped it down, blood, saliva and all, and continued. (What powers of endurance I had during those days! What enthusiasm! What a belief in the rightness of things!) I spoke even louder in spite of the pain. But still they talked and still they laughed, as though deaf with cotton in dirty ears. So I spoke with greater emotional emphasis. I closed my ears and swallowed blood until I was nauseated. The speech seemed a hundred times as long as before, but I could not leave out a single word. All had to be said, each memorized nuance considered, rendered. Nor was that all. Whenever I uttered a word of three or more syllables a group of voices would yell for me to repeat it. I used the phrase "social responsibility" and they yelled:

"What's that word you say, boy?"

"Social responsibility," I said.

"What?"

"Social . . ."

"Louder."

". . . responsibility."

"More!"

"Respon — "

"Repeat!"

" — sibility."

The room filled with the uproar of laughter until, no doubt, distracted by having to gulp down my blood, I made a mistake and yelled a phrase I had often seen denounced in newspaper editorials, heard debated in private.

"Social . . ."

"What?" they yelled.

". . . equality — "

The laughter hung smokelike in the sudden stillness. I opened my eyes, puzzled. Sounds of displeasure filled the room. The M.C. rushed forward. They shouted hostile phrases at me. But I did not understand.

A small dry mustached man in the front row blared out, "Say that slowly, son!"

"What sir?"

"What you just said!"

"Social responsibility, sir," I said.

"You weren't being smart, were you, boy?" he said, not unkindly.

"No, sir!"

"You sure that about 'equality' was a mistake?"

"Oh, yes, sir," I said. "I was swallowing blood."

"Well, you had better speak more slowly so we can understand. We mean to do right by you, but you've got to know your place at all times. All right, now, go on with your speech."

I was afraid. I wanted to leave but I wanted also to speak and I was afraid they'd snatch me down.

"Thank you, sir," I said, beginning where I had left off, and having them ignore me as before.

Yet when I finished there was a thunderous applause. I was surprised to see the superintendent come forth with a package wrapped in white tissue paper, and, gesturing for quiet, address the men.

"Gentlemen, you see that I did not overpraise this boy. He makes a good speech and some day he'll lead his people in the proper paths. And I don't have to tell you that that is important in these days and times. This is a good, smart boy, and so to encourage him in the right direction, in the name of the Board of Education I wish to present him a prize in the form of this . . ."

He paused, removing the tissue paper and revealing a gleaming calfskin brief case.

". . . in the form of this first-class article from Shad Whitmore's shop."

"Boy," he said, addressing me, "take this prize and keep it well. Consider it a badge of office. Prize it. Keep developing as you are and some day it will be filled with important papers that will help shape the destiny of your people."

I was so moved that I could hardly express my thanks. A rope of bloody saliva forming a shape like an undiscovered continent drooled upon the leather and I wiped it quickly away. I felt an importance that I had never dreamed.

"Open it and see what's inside," I was told.

My fingers a-tremble, I complied, smelling the fresh leather and finding an official-looking document inside. It was a scholarship to the state college for Negroes. My eyes filled with tears and I ran awkwardly off the floor.

I was overjoyed; I did not even mind when I discovered that the gold pieces I had scrambled for were brass pocket tokens advertising a certain make of automobile.

When I reached home everyone was excited. Next day the neighbors came to congratulate me. I even felt safe from grandfather, whose deathbed curse usually spoiled my triumphs. I stood beneath his photograph with my brief case in hand and smiled triumphantly into his stolid black peasant's face. It was a face that fascinated me. The eyes seemed to follow everywhere I went.

That night I dreamed I was at a circus with him and that he refused to laugh at the clowns no matter what they did. Then later he told me to open my brief case and read what was inside and I did, finding an official envelope stamped with the state seal; and inside the envelope I found another and another, endlessly, and I thought I would fall of weariness. "Them's years," he said. "Now open that one." And I did and in it I found an engraved document containing a short message in letters of gold. "Read it," my grandfather said. "Out loud."

"To Whom It May Concern," I intoned. "Keep This Nigger-Boy Running."

I awoke with the old man's laughter ringing in my ears.

---

1. What is the narrator's goal? Does he have more than one?
2. Where did he get the idea of this goal?
3. What was his grandfather's goal? Why? Could he substitute a better one?
4. This is the first chapter of a novel. Later in the book the narrator examines his goal and changes it. Can you predict what he will find out? What will he do?
5. Do you think this is primarily about things that could happen only to a Negro in the South? Does it have any meaning which could be applied to your life? To your goals? Has anyone ever tried to "keep you running" so that you wouldn't "get in trouble" and cause him inconvenience?
6. What is lacking in the narrator's contact with his environment? Is it true that "what you don't know won't hurt you"?
7. Is the narrator's innocence like that of the boy in Thom Gunn's poem (Unit 8)? Which characters *are* innocent in this sense? What other characters are like that in the stories you have read so far?

The Unknown Citizen

W. H. AUDEN

To JS/07/M/378
This Marble Monument Is Erected by the State

He was found by the Bureau of Statistics to be
One against whom there was no official complaint,
And all the reports on his conduct agree
That, in the modern sense of an old-fashioned word, he was a saint,
For in everything he did he served the Greater Community.
Except for the War till the day he retired
He worked in a factory and never got fired,
But satisfied his employers, Fudge Motors Inc.
Yet he wasn't a scab or odd in his views,
For his Union reports that he paid his dues,
(Our report on his Union shows it was sound)
And our Social Psychology workers found
That he was popular with his mates and liked a drink.
The Press are convinced that he bought a paper every day
And that his reactions to advertisements were normal in every way.
Policies taken out in his name prove that he was fully insured,
And his Health-card shows he was once in hospital but left it cured.
Both Producers Research and High-Grade Living declare
He was fully sensible to the advantages of the Installment Plan
And had everything necessary to the Modern Man,
A gramophone, a radio, a car and a frigidaire.
Our researchers into Public Opinion are content
That he held the proper opinions for the time of year;
When there was peace, he was for peace; when there was war, he went.
He was married and added five children to the population,
Which our Eugenist says was the right number for a parent of his generation,
And our teachers report that he never interfered with their education.
Was he free? Was he happy? The question is absurd:
Had anything been wrong, we should certainly have heard.

1. What is the purpose of serving "the Greater Community"?
2. What is the goal of the person who becomes an "unknown citizen"? Do you know a person like this whom you can use as an example? Does such a person exist?
3. What does "normal" mean?
4. What is the meaning of the line, "And our teachers report that he never interfered with their education"? Have you ever interfered with the education given you by your teachers?
5. Can you answer the question, "Was he free? Was he happy?" in specific terms? Is the question absurd?
6. Is the unknown citizen in any way like the narrator of *Invisible Man*? How?

---

1. Are these people part of "the Greater Community"? In what sense? What are their goals?
2. What do the men behind the glass barriers believe in? What reasons do you think they would give?
3. Try to identify with the man standing in the center of the picture. How do you feel?
4. Can you identify with the man behind the glass? How do you feel?
5. Why has the artist repeated each figure? What does this repetition mean in terms of goals?

PLATE XI

GOVERNMENT BUREAU: George Tooker   The Metropolitan Museum of Art, New York

Cartoon "Heritage" December 20, 1964 by Bill Mauldin from *I've Decided I Want My Seat Back* by Bill Mauldin. Copyright © 1964 by Bill Mauldin. Reprinted by permission of Harper & Row, Publishers.

12

looking at an institution

All social progress is laid to discontent.
—*Abraham Lincoln*

An institution is an important and firmly established custom, usually a part of the whole social structure. Some practices that are widespread and considered important, such as marriage, could be called both customs and institutions. Government, education, religion, business, industry, war, and the family are institutions. Changing a custom, such as the type of clothes we wear, for example, would not change our lives very much; but changing an institution, such as government or the family, would. The greatest upheavals in man's history have involved the changing of institutions: the establishment of Christianity and the other great religions, the beginnings of democracy and communism, the industrial revolution, the spread of literacy and of electronic communication, the growth of public education.

Institutions tend to preserve the beliefs, attitudes, and values of the past. Sometimes this is desirable, sometimes not. But even when change is clearly desirable, it is often very difficult to carry out. To uproot the institution of monarchy, for example, required centuries of devastating wars. And war itself, though few people would defend it as a desirable institution, continues to exist.

Nevertheless, because perceptive individuals saw that they were faulty, institutions have been changed in the past, and they will continue to be changed in the future. Since they play a large part in your life, you might well focus a part of your awareness upon institutions and your own contact with them.

class discussion

The educational system is one institution with which you have had a great deal of experience. What, exactly, are the purposes of the school? If all the schools suddenly ceased to exist – if all the school boards and departments and teachers and buildings disappeared overnight – would you replace them with an identical system? What changes would you make? Are there possibly any ways to accomplish the purposes of the school without having schools at all? In what ways might these alternatives be better? Not as good?

writing assignment

1. Choose one of the institutions with which you have had a great deal of experience: the family, the church, the school, the retail business, the farm (if you've lived or worked on one), the city (if you grew up in one).
2. Define exactly the purpose of this institution in relation to yourself. What has it provided you with? What has it taken from you? How necessary has it been to you? Give specific examples, making clear by describing actual experiences just what the institution has meant to you.
3. Now, imagine how it might have been if that institution had not existed. Imagine a substitute for it, the best you can create, which would be as different from it as possible and yet provide the same necessities.
4. What *advantages* might this new institution have offered you that the actual one did not? How might it have made some aspects of your life better?
5. Conclude with several *general* statements about the shortcomings of the present institution that might be corrected by changing some aspects of it.

class writing exercise

Begin with a thesis something like, "The institution of ______ has several disadvantages." Then from your concluding statements for the preceding writing assignment, construct topic sentences for three or four paragraphs about what these disadvantages have been for *you*. Fill the paragraphs with examples from your own experience in which you vividly describe how the institution has fallen short of your needs or desires.

alternate exercise

Write a narrative, telling the story of an especially sad, happy, or otherwise memorable experience you once had with an institution. Tell the story as completely as you can in the time you have, letting the reader share the sights, sounds, smells, and feelings you experienced. Fill your story with sensory detail as Hemingway does in "Big Two-Hearted River" (Unit 2).

The Human Factory

ALFRED KAZIN

. . . When I passed the school, I went sick with all my old fear of it. With its standard New York public-school brown brick courtyard shut in on three sides of the square and the pretentious battlements overlooking that cockpit in which I can still smell the fiery sheen of the rubber ball, it looks like a factory over which has been imposed a façade of a castle. It gave me the shivers to stand up in that courtyard again; I felt as if I had been mustered back into the service of those Friday morning "tests" that were the terror of my childhood.

It was never learning I associated with that school: only the necessity to succeed, to get ahead of the others in the daily struggle to "make a good impression" on our teachers, who grimly, wearily, and often with ill-concealed distaste watched against our relapsing into the natural savagery

---

they expected of Brownsville boys. The white, cool, thinly ruled record book sat over us from their desks all day long, and had remorselessly entered into it each day — in blue ink if we had passed, in red ink if we had not — our attendance, our conduct, our "effort," our merits and demerits; and to the last possible decimal point in calculation, our standing in an unending series of "tests" — surprise tests, daily tests, weekly tests, formal midterm tests, final tests. They never stopped trying to dig out of us whatever small morsel of fact we had managed to get down the night before. We had to prove that we were really alert, ready for anything, always in the race. That white thinly ruled record book figured in my mind as the judgment seat; the very thinness and remote blue lightness of its lines instantly showed its cold authority over me; so much space had been left on each page, columns and columns in which to note down everything about us, implacably and forever. As it lay there on a teacher's desk, I stared at it all day long with such fear and anxious propriety that I had no trouble believing God, too, did nothing but keep such record books, and that on the final day He would face me with an account in Hebrew letters whose phonetic dots and dashes looked strangely like decimal points counting up my every sinful thought on earth.

All teachers were to be respected like gods, and God Himself was the greatest of all school superintendents. Long after I had ceased to believe that our teachers could see with the back of their heads, it was still understood, by me, that they knew everything. They were the delegates of all visible and invisible power on earth — of the mothers who waited on the stoops every day after three for us to bring home tales of our daily triumphs; of the glacially remote Anglo-Saxon principal, whose very name was King; of the incalculably important Superintendent of Schools who would someday rubberstamp his name to the bottom of our diplomas in grim acknowledgment that we had, at last, given satisfaction to him, to the Board of Superintendents, and to our benefactor the City of New York — and so up and up, to the government of the United States and to the great Lord Jehovah Himself. My belief in teachers' unlimited wisdom and power rested not so much on what I saw in them — how impatient most of them looked, how wary — but on our abysmal humility, at least in those of us who were "good" boys, who proved by our ready compliance and "manners" that we wanted to get on. The road to a professional future would be shown us only as we pleased *them. Make a good impression the first day of the term, and they'll help you out. Make a bad impression, and you might as well cut your throat.* This was the first article of school folklore, whispered around the classroom the opening day of each term. You made the "good impression" by sitting firmly at your wooden desk, hands clasped; by silence for the greatest part of the live-long day; by standing up obsequiously when it was so expected of you; by sitting down noiselessly when you had answered a question; by "speaking nicely," which meant reproducing their painfully exact enunciation; by "showing manners," or an ecstatic submissiveness in all things; by outrageous flattery; by bringing little gifts at Christmas, on their birthdays, and at the end of the term – the well-known significance of these gifts being that they came not from us, but from our parents, whose eagerness in this matter showed a high level of social consideration, and thus raised our standing in turn.

It was not just our quickness and memory that were always being tested. Above all, in that word I could never hear without automatically seeing it raised before me in gold-plated letters, it was our *character.* I always felt anxious when I heard the word pronounced. Satisfactory as my "character" was, on the whole, except when I stayed too long in the playground reading; outrageously satisfactory, as I can see now, the very sound of the word as our teachers coldly gave it out from the end of their teeth, with a solemn weight on each dark syllable, immediately struck my heart cold with fear – they could not believe I really had it. Character was never something you had; it had to be trained in you, like a technique. I was never very clear about it. On our side *character* meant demonstrative obedience; but teachers already had it – how else could they have become teachers? They had it; the aloof Anglo-Saxon principal whom we remotely saw only on ceremonial occasions in the assembly was positively encased in it; it glittered off his bald head in spokes of triumphant light; the President of the United States had the greatest conceivable amount of it. Character belonged to great adults. Yet we were constantly being driven onto it; it was the great threshold we had to cross. *Alfred Kazin, having shown proficiency in his course of studies and having displayed satisfactory marks of character* . . . Thus someday the hallowed diploma, passport to my further advancement in high school. But there – I could already feel it in my bones – they would put me through even more doubting tests of character; and after that, if I should be good enough and bright enough, there would be still more. *Character* was a bitter thing, racked with my endless striving to please. The school – from every last stone in the courtyard to the battlements frowning down at me from the walls – was only the stage for a trial. I felt that the very atmosphere of learning that surrounded us was fake – that every lesson, every book, every approving smile was only a pretext for the constant probing and watching of me, that there was not a secret in me that would not be decimally measured into that white record book. All week long I lived for the blessed sound of the dismissal gong at three o'clock on Friday afternoon.

I was awed by this system, I believed in it, I respected its force. The alternative was "going bad." The school was notoriously the toughest in our tough neighborhood, and the dangers of "going bad" were constantly impressed upon me at home and in school in dark whispers of the "reform school" and in examples of boys who had been picked up for petty thievery, rape, or flinging a heavy inkwell straight into a teacher's face. Behind any failure in school yawned the great abyss of a criminal career. Every refractory attitude doomed you with the sound "Sing Sing." Anything less than absolute perfection in school always suggested to my mind that I might fall out of the daily race, be kept back in the working class forever, or — dared I think of it? — fall into the criminal class itself.

I worked on a hairline between triumph and catastrophe. Why the odds should always have felt so narrow I understood only when I realized how little my parents thought of their own lives. It was not for myself alone that I was expected to shine, but for them — to redeem the constant anxiety of their existence. I was the first American child, their offering to the strange new God; I was to be the monument of their liberation from the shame of being — what they were. And that there was shame in this was a fact that everyone seemed to believe as a matter of course. It was in the gleeful discounting of themselves — what do we know? — with which our parents greeted every fresh victory in our savage competition for "high averages," for prizes, for a few condescending words of official praise from the principal at assembly. It was in the sickening invocation of "Americanism" — the word itself accusing us of everything we apparently were not. Our families and teachers seemed tacitly agreed that we were somehow to be a little ashamed of what we were. Yet it was always hard to say why this should be so. It was certainly not — in Brownsville! — because we were Jews, or simply because we spoke another language at home, or were absent on our holy days. It was rather that a "refined," "correct," "nice" English was required of us at school that we did not naturally speak, and that our teachers could never be quite sure we would keep. This English was peculiarly the ladder of advancement. Every future young lawyer was known by it. Even the Communists and Socialists on Pitkin Avenue spoke it. It was bright and clean and polished. We were expected to show it off like a new pair of shoes. When the teacher sharply called a question out, then your name, you were expected to leap up, face the class, and eject those new words fluently off the tongue.

There was my secret ordeal: I could never say anything except in the most roundabout way; I was a stammerer. Although I knew all those new words from my private reading — I read walking in the street, to and from the Children's Library on Stone Avenue; on the fire escape and the roof; at every meal when they would let me; read even when I dressed in the morning, propping my book up against the drawers of the bureau as I pulled on my long black stockings — I could never seem to get the easiest words out with the right dispatch, and would often miserably signal from my desk that I did not know the answer rather than get up to stumble and fall and crash on every word. If, angry at always being put down as lazy or stupid, I did get up to speak, the black wooden floor would roll away under my feet, the teacher would frown at me in amazement, and in unbearable loneliness I would hear behind me the groans and laughter: *tuh-tuh-tuh-tuh*.

The word was my agony. The word that for others was so effortless and so neutral, so unburdened, so simple, so exact, I had first to meditate in advance, to see if I could make it, like a plumber fitting together odd lengths and shapes of pipe. I was always preparing words I could speak, storing them away, choosing between them. And often, when the word did come from my mouth in its great and terrible birth, quailing and bleeding as if forced through a thornbush, I would not be able to look the others in the face, and would walk out in the silence, the infinitely echoing silence behind my back, to say it all cleanly back to myself as I walked in the streets. Only when I was alone in the open air, pacing the roof with pebbles in my mouth, as I had read Demosthenes had done to cure himself of stammering; or in the street, where all words seemed to flow from the length of my stride and the color of the houses as I remembered the perfect tranquillity of a phrase in Beethoven's *Romance in F* I could sing back to myself as I walked — only then was it possible for me to speak without the infinite premeditations and strangled silences I toiled through whenever I got up at school to respond with the expected, the exact answer.

It troubled me that I could speak in the fullness of my own voice only when I was alone on the streets, walking about. There was something unnatural about it; unbearably isolated. I was not like the others! I was not like the others! At midday, every freshly shocking Monday noon, they sent me away to a speech clinic in a school in East New York, where I sat in a circle of lispers and cleft palates and foreign accents holding a mirror before my lips and rolling difficult sounds over and over. To be sent there in the full light of the opening week, when everyone else was at school or going about his business, made me feel as if I had been expelled from the great normal body of humanity. I would gobble down my lunch on my way to the speech clinic and rush back to the school in time to make up for the classes I had lost. One day, one unforgettable dread day, I stopped to catch my breath on a corner of Sutter Avenue, near the wholesale fruit markets, where an old drugstore rose up over a great flight of steps. In the window were dusty urns of colored water floating off iron chains; cardboard placards advertising hairnets, Ex-Lax; a great illustrated medical chart headed THE HUMAN FACTORY, which showed the exact course a mouthful of food follows as it falls from chamber to chamber of the body. I hadn't meant to stop there at all, only to catch my breath; but I so hated the speech clinic that I thought I would delay my arrival for a few minutes by eating my lunch on the steps. When I took the sandwich out of my bag, two bitterly hard pieces of hard salami slipped out of my hand and fell through a grate onto a hill of dust below the steps. I remember how sickeningly vivid an odd thread of hair looked on the salami, as if my lunch were turning stiff with death. The factory whistles called their short, sharp blasts stark through the middle of noon, beating at me where I sat outside the city's magnetic circle. I had never known, I knew instantly I would never in my heart again submit to, such wild passive despair as I felt at that moment, sitting on the steps before THE HUMAN FACTORY, where little robots gathered and shoveled the food from chamber to chamber of the body. They had put me out into the streets, I thought to myself; with their mirrors and their everlasting pulling at me to imitate their effortless bright speech and their stupefaction that a boy could stammer and stumble on every other English word he carried on his head, they had put me out into the streets, had left me high and dry on the steps of that drugstore staring at the remains of my lunch turning black and grimy in the dust.

---

1. What institution is Alfred Kazin examining? Is it only the school, or does his examination go beyond the school?
2. What things did the school teach Kazin? What things did it judge him by? Was there any conflict between these?
3. The author turned out to be both learned and successful. Do you think this had to do with what he learned in school, or with his feeling rejected by the school, or both? Try to analyze his experience and answer as clearly as possible, separating the effects of the two. The next to last sentence of the essay might provide a clue.
4. Have you had any experiences in school similar to Kazin's? What do you think the effect of these experiences has been?

The Death of the Ball Turret Gunner

RANDALL JARRELL

From my mother's sleep I fell into the State,
And I hunched in its belly till my wet fur froze.
Six miles from earth, loosed from its dream of life,
I woke to black flak and the nightmare fighters.
When I died they washed me out of the turret with a hose.

---

1. A "ball turret" was a spherical revolving machine-gun turret on the underside of the Boeing B-17 bomber, extensively used in World War II. The gunner there was in an especially vulnerable position since fighters usually attack from behind and underneath. The gunner, then, in his fur-lined jacket, is hunched in the belly of the plane. What does the plane stand for? What was the gunner born into?
2. There are two images in the poem, one of birth and the other of abortion. From what is the gunner aborted?
3. Coldness is emphasized by the rhyming of "froze" and "hose," the only end rhyme in the poem. What is it that is cold? What attitude of the institution toward the individual is represented by this coldness?
4. In the second line, the gunner likens himself to a cold, frightened young animal. Why?
5. What institution is being examined in this poem?

---

1. At first glance, the child in this painting seems to be a victim of bombing, and the artist probably meant for us to have this first impression. However, we see upon closer inspection that the debris is not that of war. What does it seem to be?
2. What is the significance of the oil tanks in the background? Of the appearance of the child's skin?
3. What is almost entirely missing from the landscape the child is in? How would you describe this landscape? What has made it that way?
4. What institution is the artist commenting upon? What is he saying about it? What is he comparing it with?

PLATE XII

ECHO OF A SCREAM: David Alfaro Siqueiros Collection, The Museum of Modern Art, New York; gift of Edward M. M. Warburg

From *Dreams of Glory,* by William Steig. Copyright 1953 by William Steig. Reprinted by permission of Alfred A. Knopf, Inc.

13

reliving a past experience

To be able to enjoy one's past life is to live twice. —*Martial*

In several of the previous units you have focused your awareness on *here and now;* in Unit 5 you extended your awareness to faraway things, and in Unit 11 you considered future possibilities. Another dimension of awareness remains to be explored: your own past.

Most of us at various times in our lives become involved in school, in work, in emotional problems, or in striving toward goals, and we forget what it is that we really enjoy most in life. In Unit 6 we saw Mrs. Ormsby (*The Ram in the Thicket*) and Flick Webb ("Ex-Basketball Player"), two people who seem to have become "hung up" on things that are not very important so that their enjoyment of life has been restricted; in "Big Two-Hearted River" (Unit 2) and "The Second Tree from the Corner" (Unit 4) we saw two people who succeeded in rediscovering enjoyment.

What kind of experience do you really enjoy most? One place to look for clues is in the pleasant memories of your childhood. Your past is part of you.

class discussion

What experiences did you enjoy most when you were a child — say, before the age of twelve? Try to explain *why* you enjoyed them. Do you have any equivalent experiences today which give you the same kind of enjoyment?

writing assignment

1. Spend an hour, in a quiet place, writing down all the details you can about the most pleasant childhood experience you can remember.
2. Do not worry about order; just write down things as you recall them. Concentrate on sensory data: colors, textures, sounds, smells, bodily sensations.
3. Put everything in the *present tense,* as though it were happening to you *here and now*. Begin each sentence with an expression such as "I see," "I feel," "I smell," etc.
4. Exhaust your memory of the experience, down to the most trivial detail. You should have several pages when you are through.

class writing exercise

Look over the material you have gathered for the previous writing assignment. See if you can find a *thesis* — a generalization about what these details of experience have in common to make them pleasant and memorable. Then organize your material into an essay built around that thesis. Write all of it in the *past* tense. Use as much sensory detail as you can.

Memories of a Missouri Farm

MARK TWAIN

It was a heavenly place for a boy, that farm of my uncle John's. The house was a double log one with a spacious floor (roofed in) connecting it with the kitchen. In the summer the table was set in the middle of that shady and breezy floor, and the sumptuous meals – well, it makes me cry to think of them. Fried chicken, roast pig, wild and tame turkeys, ducks and geese, venison just killed, squirrels, rabbits, pheasants, partridges, prairie-chickens, biscuits, hot batter-cakes, hot buckwheat cakes, hot "wheat bread," hot rolls, hot corn pone; fresh corn boiled on the ear, succotash, butter-beans, string-beans, tomatoes, peas, Irish potatoes, sweet potatoes; buttermilk, sweet milk; "clabber"; watermelons, muskmelons, cantaloupes – all fresh from the garden – apple pie, peach pie, pumpkin pie, apple dumplings, peach cobbler – I can't remember the rest.

The farm-house stood in the middle of a very large yard and the yard was fenced on three sides with rails and on the rear side with high palings; against these stood the smoke-house; beyond the palings was the orchard; beyond the orchard were the Negro quarter and the tobacco fields. The front yard was entered over a stile made of sawed-off logs of graduated heights; I do not remember any gate. In a corner of the front yard were a dozen lofty hickory trees and a dozen black walnuts, and in the nutting season riches were to be gathered there.

Down a piece, abreast the house, stood a little log cabin against the rail fence; and there the woody hill fell sharply away, past the barns, the corn-crib, the stables, and the tobacco-curing house, to a limpid brook which sang along over its gravelly bed and curved and frisked in and out and here and there and yonder in the deep shade of overhanging foliage and vines – a divine place for wading, and it had swimming-pools too, which were forbidden to us and therefore much frequented by us. For we were little Christian children and had early been taught the value of forbidden fruit.

In the little log cabin lived a bedridden white-headed slave woman whom we visited daily and looked upon with awe, for we believed she was upward of a thousand years old and had talked with Moses. The younger Negroes credited these statistics and had furnished them to us in good faith. We accommodated all the details which came to us about her, and so we believed that she had lost her health in the long desert trip coming out of Egypt and had never been able to get it back again. She had a round bald place on the crown of her head, and we used to creep around and gaze at it in reverent silence and reflect that it was caused by fright through seeing Pharaoh drowned. We called her "Aunt" Hannah, Southern fashion. She was superstitious, like the other Negroes; also, like them, she was deeply religious. Like them, she had great faith in prayer and employed it in all ordinary exigencies, but not in cases where a dead certainty of result was urgent. Whenever witches were around she tied up the remnant of her wool in little tufts with white thread, and this promptly made the witches impotent.

All the Negroes were friends of ours and with those of our own age we were in effect comrades. I say in effect, using the phrase as a modification. We were comrades and yet not comrades; color and condition interposed a subtle line which both parties were conscious of and which rendered complete fusion impossible. We had a faithful and affectionate good friend, ally, and adviser in "Uncle Dan'l," a middle-aged slave whose head was the best one in the Negro quarter, whose sympathies were wide and warm, and whose heart was honest and simple and knew no guile. He has served me well these many, many years. I have not seen him for more than half a century, and yet spiritually I have had his welcome company a good part of that time and have staged him in books under his own name and as Jim and carted him all around, to Hannibal, down the Mississippi on a raft, and even across the Desert of Sahara in a balloon — and he has endured it all with patience and friendliness and loyalty which were his birthright. It was on the farm that I got my strong liking for his race and my appreciation of certain of its fine qualities. This feeling and this estimate have stood the test of sixty years and more, and have suffered no impairment. The black face is as welcome to me now as it was then.

In my school-boy days I had no aversion to slavery. I was not aware that there was anything wrong about it. No one arraigned it in my hearing; the local papers said nothing against it; the local pulpit taught us that God approved it, that it was a holy thing, and that the doubter need only look in the Bible if he wished to settle his mind — and then the texts were read aloud to us to make the matter sure; if the slaves themselves had an aversion to slavery, they were wise and said nothing. In Hannibal we seldom saw a slave misused; on the farm, never.

There was, however, one small incident of my boyhood days which touched this matter and it must have meant a good deal to me or it would not have stayed in my memory, clear and sharp, vivid and shadowless, all these slow-drifting years. We had a little slave boy whom we had hired from some one, there in Hannibal. He was from the Eastern Shore of Maryland and had been brought away from his family and his friends, halfway across the American continent, and sold. He was a cheery spirit, innocent and gentle, and the noisiest creature that ever was perhaps. All day long he was singing, whistling, yelling, whooping, laughing — it was maddening, devastating, unendurable. At last, one day, I lost all my temper and went raging to my mother and said Sandy had been singing for an hour without a single break, and I couldn't stand it, and *wouldn't* she please shut him up. The tears came into her eyes and her lip trembled, and she said something like this:

"Poor thing, when he sings it shows that he is not remembering, and that comforts me; but when he is still I am afraid he is thinking and I cannot bear it. He will never see his mother again; if he can sing, I must not hinder it but be thankful for it. If you were older, you would understand me; then that friendless child's noise would make you glad."

It was a simple speech and made up of small words but it went home, and Sandy's noise was not a trouble to me any more. She never used large words but she had a natural gift for making small ones do effective work. She lived to reach the neighborhood of ninety years and was capable with her tongue to the last, especially when a meanness or an injustice roused her spirit. She has come handy to me several times in my books, where she figures as Tom Sawyer's Aunt Polly. I fitted her out with a dialect and tried to think up other improvements for her, but did not find any. I used Sandy once, also; it was in *Tom Sawyer*. I tried to get him to whitewash the fence but it did not work. I do not remember what name I called him by in the book.

I can see the farm yet with perfect clearness. I can see all its belongings, all its details: the family room of the house with a "trundle" bed in one corner and a spinning-wheel in another, a wheel whose rising and falling wail, heard from a distance, was the mournfulest of all sounds to me and made me homesick and low-spirited and filled my atmosphere with the wandering spirits of the dead; the vast fireplace, piled high on winter nights with flaming hickory logs from whose ends a sugary sap bubbled out but did not go to waste, for we scraped it off and ate it; the lazy cat spread out on the rough hearth-stones; the drowsy dogs braced against the jambs and blinking; my aunt in one chimney corner, knitting; my uncle in the other, smoking his corn-cob pipe; the slick and carpetless oak floor faintly mirroring the dancing flame-tongues and freckled with black indentations where fire-coals had popped out and died a leisurely death; half a dozen children romping in the background twilight; split-bottomed chairs here and there, some with rockers; a cradle, out of service but waiting with confidence; in the early cold mornings a snuggle of children in shirts and chemises occupying the hearth-stone and procrastinating — they could not bear to leave that comfortable place and go out on the windswept floor-space between the house and kitchen where the general tin basin stood, and wash.

Along outside of the front fence ran the country road, dusty in the summertime and a good place for snakes — they liked to lie in it and sun themselves; when they were rattlesnakes or puff adders, we killed them; when they were black snakes or racers or belonged to the fabled "hoop" breed, we fled, without shame; when they were "house-snakes" or "garters" we carried them home and put them in Aunt Patsy's work-basket for a surprise; for she was prejudiced against snakes and always when she took the basket in her lap and they began to climb out of it, it disordered her mind. She never could seem to get used to them, her opportunities went for nothing. And she was always cold toward bats, too, and could not bear them; and yet I think a bat is as friendly a bird as there is. My mother was Aunt Patsy's sister and had the same wild superstitions. A bat is beautifully soft and silky; I do not know any creature that is pleasanter to the touch or is more grateful for caressings, if offered in the right spirit. I know all about these coleoptera because our great cave, three miles below Hannibal, was multitudinously stocked with them and often I brought them home to amuse my mother with. It was easy to manage if it was a school-day, because then I had ostensibly been to school and hadn't any bats. She was not a suspicious person but full of trust and confidence, and when I said, "There's something in my coat-pocket for you," she would put her hand in. But she always took it out again, herself; I didn't have to tell her. It was remarkable, the way she couldn't learn to like private bats. The more experience she had, the more she could not change her views.

I think she was never in the cave in her life; but everybody else went there. Many excursion parties came from considerable distances up and down the river to visit the cave. It was miles in extent and was a tangled wilderness of narrow and lofty clefts and passages. It was an easy place to get lost in; anybody could do it, including the bats. I got lost in it myself, along with a lady, and our last candle burned down to almost nothing before we glimpsed the search-party's lights winding about in the distance.

"Injun Joe," the half-breed, got lost in there once and would have starved to death if the bats had run short. But there was no chance of that, there were myriads of them. He told me all his story. In the book called *Tom Sawyer* I starved him entirely to death in the cave but that was in the interest of art: it never happened. "General" Gaines, who was our first town drunkard before Jimmy Finn got the place, was lost in there for the space of a week and finally pushed his handkerchief out of a hole in a hilltop near Saverton, several miles down the river from the cave's mouth, and somebody saw it and dug him out. There is nothing the matter with his statistics except the handkerchief. I knew him for years and he hadn't any. But it could have been his nose. That would attract attention.

The cave was an uncanny place for it contained a corpse, the corpse of a young girl of fourteen. It was in a glass cylinder inclosed in a copper one which was suspended from a rail which bridged a narrow passage. The body was preserved in alcohol, and it was said that loafers and rowdies used to drag it up by the hair and look at the dead face. The girl was the daughter of a St. Louis surgeon of extraordinary ability and wide celebrity. He was an eccentric man and did many strange things. He put the poor thing in that forlorn place himself.

II

Beyond the road where the snakes sunned themselves was a dense young thicket, and through it a dim-lighted path led a quarter of a mile; then out of the dimness one emerged abruptly upon a level great prairie which was covered with wild strawberry plants, vividly starred with prairie pinks, and walled in on all sides by forests. The strawberries were fragrant and fine and in the season we were generally there in the crisp freshness of the early morning, while the dew-beads still sparkled upon the grass and the woods were ringing with the first songs of the birds.

Down the forest-slopes to the left were the swings. They were made of bark stripped from hickory saplings. When they became dry they were dangerous. They usually broke when a child was forty feet in the air, and this was why so many bones had to be mended every year. I had no ill luck myself, but none of my cousins escaped. There were eight of them and at one time and another they broke fourteen arms among them. But it cost next to nothing, for the doctor worked by the year — twenty-five dollars for the whole family. I remember two of the Florida doctors, Chowning and Meredith. They not only tended an entire family for twenty-five dollars a year but furnished the medicines themselves. Good measure, too. Only the largest persons could hold a whole dose. Castor oil was the principal beverage. The dose was a half a dipperful, with half a dipperful of New Orleans molasses added to help it down and make it taste good, which it never did. The next standby was calomel, the next rhubarb, and the next jalap. Then they bled the patient and put mustard plasters on him. It was a dreadful system and yet the death-rate was not heavy. The calomel was nearly sure to salivate the patient and cost him some of his teeth. There were no dentists. When teeth became touched with decay or were otherwise ailing, the doctor knew of but one thing to do: he fetched his tongs and dragged them out. If the jaw remained, it was not his fault. Doctors were not called in cases of ordinary illness; the family grandmother attended to those. Every old woman was a doctor and gathered her own medicines in the woods, and knew how to compound doses that would stir the vitals of a cast-iron dog. And then there was the "Indian doctor," a grave savage, remnant of his tribe, deeply read in the mysteries of nature and the secret properties of herbs; and most backwoodsmen had high faith in his powers and could tell of wonderful cures achieved by him. In Mauritius, away off yonder in the solitudes of the Indian Ocean, there is a person who answers to our Indian doctor of the old times. He is a Negro and has had no teaching as a doctor, yet there is one disease which he is master of and can cure and the doctors can't. They send for him when they have a case. It is a child's disease of a strange and deadly sort, and the Negro cures it with an herb-medicine which he makes himself, from a prescription which has come down to him from his father and grandfather. He will not let anyone see it. He keeps the secret of its components to himself, and it is feared that he will die without divulging it; then there will be consternation in Mauritius. I was told these things by the people there, in 1896.

We had the "faith doctor" too, in those early days, a woman. Her specialty was toothache. She was a farmer's old wife and lived five miles from Hannibal. She would lay her hand on the patient's jaw and say, "Believe!" and the cure was prompt. Mrs. Utterback. I remember her very well. Twice I rode out there behind my mother, horseback, and saw the cure performed. My mother was the patient.

Dr. Meredith removed to Hannibal by and by, and was our family physician there, and saved my life several times. Still, he was a good man and meant well. Let it go.

I was always told that I was a sickly and precarious and tiresome and uncertain child, and lived mainly on allopathic medicines during the first seven years of my life. I asked my mother about this in her old age — she was in her eighty-eighth year — and said:

"I suppose that during all that time you were uneasy about me?"

"Yes, the whole time."

"Afraid I wouldn't live?"

After a reflective pause, ostensibly to think out the facts, "No — afraid you would."

The country school-house was three miles from my uncle's farm. It stood in a clearing in the woods and would hold about twenty-five boys and girls. We attended the school with more or less regularity once or twice a week in summer, walking to it in the cool of the morning by the forest paths and back in the gloaming at the end of the day. All the pupils brought their dinners in baskets — corn dodger, buttermilk, and other good things — and sat in the shade of the trees at noon and ate them. It is the part of my education which I look back upon with the most satisfaction. My first visit to the school was when I was seven. A strapping girl of fifteen, in the customary sunbonnet and calico dress, asked me if I "used tobacco," meaning did I chew it. I said no. It roused her scorn. She reported me to all the crowd, and said:

"Here is a boy seven years old who can't chew tobacco."

By the looks and comments which this produced I realized that I was a degraded object, and was cruelly ashamed of myself. I determined to reform. But I only made myself sick; I was not able to learn to chew tobacco. I learned to smoke fairly well but that did not conciliate anybody and I remained a poor thing, and characterless. I longed to be respected but I never was able to rise. Children have but little charity for each other's defects.

As I have said, I spent some part of every year at the farm until I was twelve or thirteen years old. The life which I led there with my cousins was full of charm and so is the memory of it yet. I can call back the solemn twilight and mystery of the deep woods, the earthy smells, the faint odors of the wild flowers, the sheen of rain-washed foliage, the rattling clatter of drops when the wind shook the trees, the far-off hammering of woodpeckers and the muffled drumming of wood-pheasants in the remoteness of the forest, the snapshot glimpses of disturbed wild creatures scurrying through the grass — I can call it all back and make it as real as it ever was, and as blessed. I can call back the prairie, and its loneliness and peace, and a vast hawk hanging motionless in the sky with his wings spread wide and the blue of the vault showing through the fringe of their end-feathers. I can see the woods in their autumn dress, the oaks purple, the hickories washed with gold, the maples and the sumachs luminous with crimson fires, and I can hear the rustle made by the fallen leaves as we plowed through them. I can see the blue clusters of wild grapes hanging amongst the foliage of the saplings, and I remember the taste of them and the smell. I know how the wild blackberries looked and how they tasted; and the same with the pawpaws, the hazelnuts, and the persimmons; and I can feel the thumping rain upon my head of hickory-nuts and walnuts when we were out in the frosty dawn to scramble for them with the pigs, and the gusts of wind loosed them and sent them down. I know the stain of blackberries and how pretty it is, and I know the stain of walnut hulls and how little it minds soap and water, also what grudged experience it had of either of them. I know the taste of maple sap and when to gather it, and how to arrange the troughs and the delivery tubes, and how to boil down the juice, and how to hook the sugar after it is made; also how much better hooked sugar tastes than any that is honestly come by, let bigots say what they will.

I know how a prize watermelon looks when it is sunning its fat rotundity among pumpkin vines and "simblins"; I know how to tell when it is ripe without "plugging" it. I know how inviting it looks when it is cooling itself in a tub of water under the bed, waiting; I know how it looks when it lies on the table in the sheltered great floor-space between house and kitchen, and the children gathered for the sacrifice and their mouths watering. I know the crackling sound it makes when the carving knife enters its end and I can see the split fly along in front of the blade as the knife cleaves its way to the other end; I can see its halves fall apart and display the rich red meat and the black seeds, and the heart standing up, a luxury fit for the elect. I know how a boy looks behind a yard-long slice of that melon and I know how he feels, for I have been there. I know the taste of the watermelon which has been honestly come by and I know the taste of the watermelon which has been acquired by art. Both taste good but the experienced know which tastes best.

I know the look of green apples and peaches and pears on the trees, and I know how entertaining they are when they are inside of a person. I know how ripe ones look when they are piled in pyramids under the trees, and how pretty they are and how vivid their colors. I know how a frozen apple looks in a barrel down cellar in the wintertime, and how hard it is to bite and how the frost makes the teeth ache, and yet how good it is notwithstanding. I know the disposition of elderly people to select the specked apples for the children and I once knew ways to beat the game. I know the look of an apple that is roasting and sizzling on a hearth on a winter's evening, and I know the comfort that comes of eating it hot, along with some sugar and a drench of cream. I know the delicate art and mystery of so cracking hickory-nuts and walnuts on a flatiron with a hammer that the kernels will be delivered whole, and I know how the nuts, taken in conjunction with winter apples, cider, and doughnuts, make old people's old tales and old jokes sound fresh and crisp and enchanting, and juggle an evening away before you know what went with the time. I know the look of Uncle Dan'l's kitchen as it was on privileged nights when I was a child, and I can see the white and black children grouped on the hearth, with the firelight playing on their faces and the shadows flickering upon the walls clear back toward the cavernous gloom of the rear, and I can hear Uncle Dan'l telling the immortal tales which Uncle Remus Harris was to gather into his book and charm the world with, by and by. And I can feel again the creepy joy which quivered through me when the time for the ghost story was reached—and the sense of regret too which came over me, for it was always the last story of the evening and there was nothing between it and the unwelcome bed.

I can remember the bare wooden stairway in my uncle's house and the turn to the left above the landing, and the rafters and the slanting roof over my bed, and the squares of moonlight on the floor and the white cold world of snow outside, seen through the curtainless window. I can remember the howling of the wind and the quaking of the house on stormy nights, and how snug and cozy one felt under the blankets, listening; and how the powdery snow used to sift in around the sashes and lie in little ridges on the floor, and make the place look chilly in the morning and curb the wild desire to get up — in case there was any. I can remember how very dark that room was in the dark of the moon, and how pleasant it was to lie and listen to it an denjoy the white splendor dent away in the night, and forgotten sins came flocking out of the secret chambers of the memory and wanted a hearing; and how ill-chosen the time seemed for this kind of business and how dismal was the hoo-hooing of the owl and the wailing of the wolf, sent mourning by on the night wind.

I remember the raging of the rain on that roof, summer nights, and how pleasant it was to lie and listen to it and enjoy the white splendor of the lightning and the majestic booming and crashing of the thunder. It was a very satisfactory room, and there was a lightning rod which was reachable from the window, an adorable and skittish thing to climb up and down, summer nights when there were duties on hand of a sort to make privacy desirable.

I remember the 'coon and 'possum hunts, nights, with the Negroes, and the long marches through the black gloom of the woods and the excitement which fired everybody when the distant bay of an experienced dog announced that the game was treed; then the wild scramblings and stumblings through briers and bushes and over roots to get to the spot; then the lighting of a fire and the felling of the tree, the joyful frenzy of the dogs and the Negroes, and the weird picture it all made in the red glare — I remember it all well, and the delight that everyone got out of it, except the 'coon.

I remember the pigeon seasons, when the birds would come in millions and cover the trees and by their weight break down the branches. They were clubbed to death with sticks; guns were not necessary and were not used. I remember the squirrel hunts and prairie-chicken hunts and wild-turkey hunts, and all that; and how we turned out, mornings, while it was still dark to go on these expeditions, and how chilly and dismal it was and how often I regretted that I was well enough to go. A toot on a tin horn brought twice as many dogs as were needed, and in their happiness they raced and scampered about and knocked small people down and made no end of unnecessary noise. At the word, they vanished away toward the woods and we drifted silently after them in the melancholy gloom. But presently the gray dawn stole over the world, the birds piped up, then the sun rose and poured light and comfort all around, everything was fresh and dewy and fragrant, and life was a boon again. After three hours of tramping we arrived back wholesomely tired, overladen with game, very hungry, and just in time for breakfast.

1. What experiences does Mark Twain seem to remember with the most pleasure? Are they unusual experiences? Have you had any of them yourself? Which ones?
2. Is Mark Twain's memory largely visual, or does he remember things experienced with the other senses? Are any of the senses neglected?
3. Does he see his childhood through "rose-colored glasses"? Can you guess some unpleasant experiences he leaves out?
4. Alfred Kazin's memories of his school are unpleasant. What does Mark Twain say about his school?
5. Do you feel that Mark Twain, writing in middle age, was still able to enjoy some of the youthful experiences he describes? Which ones?
6. What are some of the things you enjoyed as a child that you still enjoy? What are some you can no longer enjoy?

Grinding Scythe

ROBERT P. TRISTRAM COFFIN

There was the boy, the grindstone, and the man —
That was all there was to all the world.
The man was only hands and did not count,
His mind was nowhere else but in his hands.
The boy went over double, down, back up,
And over the same way he just had gone,
The wheel went over with him. The man ground,
Holding the scythe hard, slantwise on the stone.
The boy was hot inside his clothes, the air
Did not seem able to go up inside
His breeches' legs. Maybe the hotness there
Drove it out. The seam his breeches had
Was threatening to make two out of the boy,
And that would be more than his folks could stand!

The man was bearing down, the gray stone blued
To glassy tracks of dryness as the scythe
Slid on and hissed, and made the sandy sound
That put the boy's teeth on a crinkly edge
And made ice down his spine in mid-July.

Somewhere, a world or two away, the flocks
Of sandpeeps turned to silver as they wheeled,
A brook came down through beechwoods, and cool birds
Sounded double under roofs of leaves.
The brook fell to the meadow where small stones
Had rainbows on them, and a dragonfly
Flew and flew, and stood still as he flew,
And there were newts' eggs, maybe, in the pool,
And if you drank them up, with your hot mouth
Touching on the wrinkle of clear water,
There would be trouble, so your elders said.
Out in the sun beyond, the thatch ran azure
When the wind went over, and black beads
With gold on them, which were the meadow spiders,
Hung on a nothing stretched from grass to grass.
But mostly it was breeze and smell of water,
The sweet stream cutting dark, deep underground,
Salt pools where the blunt minnows bumped your legs.
Breeze and the coolness out there, wave on wave.

The heat came from the stone the boy turned round.
The man pressed down too hard. He was no longer
A man the boy made friends with, but just man —
Any man at all — and so he hated
All boys for being boys and going to play.
It must be time for water from the can,
And that would give the boy a chance to breathe.
The man was big and cool as cucumbers
In legs and arms, the hotness of the stone
Did not go up his arms to him at all,
Any boy would hate a man for that.
The wheel was much too big upon one side,
It made the turning boy hump the same way.

The aeon ended, and the man let up
So quick the boy went round and round all wild.
He tipped the can and let the rusty water
Run round the whirling stone and up again.
The grinder tried his scythe's edge on his thumb,
Shook his head, and bent to grind some more,
The aeon settled back, the heat returned.
The boy went careful, for a sudden hitch
Might trip the blade and put a notch in it
Would take two aeons more to straighten out,
And words as hot as hornets in the hay
Would come singing out of the cool man.
Off they went, the grindstone and the boy.
It was the fussy convex side. That took
Twice as many turns the other did,
The ridge in places on it was worn through
By other boys before his time. A locust
Screamed above the hissing of the steel
And went up screaming out of sound of sound.
You had to make the small teeth on each side
Run in opposite ways, the boy knew how,
The man had never dreamed the boy had learned
About it. The boy hated him for that.
It was ticklish, working round the point,
But that was nothing to the getting in
Along the V-shaped heel, with every chance
The boy might be well speared who turned the stone.
It took pains to get a scythe ground right.

The trees, the pool, the birds flowed out of mind,
The world turned more and more into a flat,
Lop-sided thing, all grit, with desperate streams
Trying to drop off its under side
But being carried up and round once more.
Maybe, there had been cool calls of birds
Echoing through high leaves and daisies, wide
As eyes of cows, in thousands up a hill,
But now there was a heat, a sanded sound
That set the teeth on edge, and blistered hands.

The man stood up, the boy went hurtling round.
"There, Son, maybe that edge will last two swaths."

The boy sat down and felt the waves of heat
Ripple off his mind. The man went down
Along the field, legs wide, on shuffling feet,
All arms and back and bigness of a man.
The daisies bowed before him, fell together,
There was the long, cool, whisper of the scythe.

---

1. Here we have a child's view of the adult world of work. What does he think of it? To what degree do you think he is right?
2. Are there any lines which bring out the stupidity, inefficiency, or insensitivity of adults? Which ones?
3. Looking at things from the boy's view, what is the significance of the next to last line, "The daisies bowed before him, fell together"? Have daisies been mentioned before?
4. Can you recall any early experiences of your own in which the adult working world seemed foolish? Do you think you were right or wrong?

---

1. As in Coffin's "Grinding Scythe," again we see the child looking at an aspect of the adult world and finding it strange. What aspect of the adult world does the "family tree" in this painting represent?
2. What is a family tree? Does this picture show a family tree in the usual sense? What is different about it?
3. A number of symbols appear in the "tree." What do they represent? What differences are there between the symbols at the bottom of the tree and those at the top?
4. Can you remember how you thought about your ancestors when you were a small child? Does Bohrod represent any of the impressions you had? How would you change the picture to represent your own impressions better?
5. Does the picture show the "family tree" from a child's point of view entirely, or do you find the artist expressing some adult ideas as well? What ideas?

PLATE XIII

FAMILY TREE: Aaron Bohrod   Courtesy of Abbott Laboratories and the artist

14

searching for meaning

> We that acquaint ourselves with ev'ry
> zone,
> And pass both tropics, and behold each
> pole,
> When we come home are to ourselves
> unknown,
> And unacquainted still with our own soul.
>
> —*Sir John Davies*

You may never have asked yourself in so many words, "Who am I? What is the meaning of my life?" Nevertheless, such questions are probably in the back of your mind, and your own picture of yourself has no doubt influenced many of your actions. Without putting it in words, we all ask now and then, "Is this something I should do? Does it fit my picture of myself?"

The existentialists, a famous and influential group of modern philosophers, say that the meaning of your life is the sum total of your actions, added up at the moment of your death. It does not matter, they say, what your thoughts and feelings have been. It is your actions that count; you *are* the total of your actions. What actions would you like to have accomplished by the end of your life? Asking questions like this is one way to focus on what your life means to you.

So that your focus will not be too goal-oriented, however, you might also ask, "What would I like to have *experienced* by the end of my life?" At this point it might help you to go back over your explorations of experience in the previous assignments in this book. Have you found pleasure or value in cultivating your perception of things, thoughts, emotions, and people? Have your brief looks at customs and institutions helped you to see yourself in relation to others? Have you gained any insights into what things you enjoy or value most? Keep such questions in mind as you do the following assignments.

class discussion

What do you want to accomplish and experience before the end of your life? Be prepared to defend your answer as your classmates comment upon it.

If someone asked you, quite seriously, "Who *are* you?" how would you try to answer him? How would you try to define yourself? How are you different from others?

writing assignment

1. Imagine yourself at the age of seventy. Imagine that you have lived essentially the kind of life you now think you would like to live. Write down, as though they had actually taken place in the past, all of the experiences and accomplishments you hope for in a long life. Do not attempt any order; just write things down as you think of them.
2. Use the past tense throughout, beginning your sentences something like this: "At the age of thirty-six I . . . ."
3. Include everything you really want to do, even though you may think it unlikely that you will be able to do it. If you want to explore the headwaters of the Amazon, then tell about how you managed to do it. But be specific! If you don't know where the headwaters of the Amazon are, you will have a hard time convincing us that you really want to go there.
4. Include little things you would like to do as well as big things. If one of your ambitions is to learn to bake a good apple pie, then tell how you did it.
5. After each item, tell us *why* you wanted to do this or experience this, and tell us what satisfaction you got from it.
6. Continue until you have described a full life, and until you have exhausted all the ideas you have at present.

class writing exercise

Look over the material from the last writing assignment. Which are the most important accomplishments and experiences? Put a number 1 beside each of these. Mark those next in importance with a number 2, and so on until you are down to number 4 or 5 for the least important items.

Now, continuing to imagine that you are seventy years old, explain who you are in terms of your actions, organizing your essay around the idea of importance. Your thesis might be something like, "I am a person who has done many good things in my life, some more important than others."

Which are you going to tell about first, the most important or the least important?

If you begin with the most important things, your essay will run down as it approaches its end and become less and less interesting. It will be *anticlimactic*, like a television Western in which the hero is rescued from danger at the beginning and nothing extraordinary happens during the rest of the show. What you want is the opposite. You want your essay to work up to a *climax* near the end, so that your reader will read with increasing interest. Save your most important points for last.

Just one caution: you know, by now, how much you can write in the time you have. Don't run out of time before you reach your important points! And in explaining *all* your points, *don't forget to be specific.*

A Mother's Tale

JAMES AGEE

The calf ran up the hill as fast as he could and stopped sharp. "Mama!" he cried, all out of breath. "What *is* it! What are they *doing!* Where are they *going!*"

Other spring calves came galloping too.

They all were looking up at her and awaiting her explanation, but she looked out over their excited eyes. As she watched the mysterious and majestic thing they had never seen before, her own eyes became even more than ordinarily still, and during the considerable moment before she answered, she scarcely heard their urgent questioning.

Far out along the autumn plain, beneath the sloping light, an immense drove of cattle moved eastward. They went at a walk, not very fast, but faster than they could imaginably enjoy. Those in front were compelled by those behind; those at the rear, with few exceptions, did their best to keep up; those who were locked within the herd could no more help moving than the particles inside a falling rock. Men on horses rode ahead, and alongside, and behind, or spurred their horses intensely back and forth, keeping the pace steady, and the herd in shape; and from man to man a dog sped back and forth incessantly as a shuttle, barking, incessantly, in a hysterical voice. Now and then one of the men shouted fiercely, and this like the shrieking of the dog was tinily audible above a low and awesome sound which seemed to come not from the multitude of hooves but from the center of the world, and above the sporadic bawlings and bellowings of the herd.

From the hillside this tumult was so distant that it only made more delicate the prodigious silence in which the earth and sky were held; and, from the hill, the sight was as modest as its sound. The herd was virtually hidden in the dust it raised, and could be known, in general, only by the horns which pricked this flat sunlit dust like little briars. In one place a twist of the air revealed the trembling fabric of many backs; but it was only along the near edge of the mass that individual animals were discernible, small in a driven frieze, walking fast, stumbling and recovering, tossing their armed heads, or opening their skulls heavenward in one of those cries which reached the hillside long after the jaws were shut.

From where she watched, the mother could not be sure whether there were any she recognized. She knew that among them there must be a son of hers; she had not seen him since some previous spring, and she would not be seeing him again. Then the cries of the young ones impinged on her bemusement: "Where are they going?"

She looked into their ignorant eyes.

"Away," she said.

"Where?" they cried. "Where? Where?" her own son cried again.

She wondered what to say.

"On a long journey."

"But where *to*?" they shouted. "Yes, where *to*?" her son exclaimed, and she could see that he was losing his patience with her, as he always did when he felt she was evasive.

"I'm not sure," she said.

Their silence was so cold that she was unable to avoid their eyes for long.

"Well, not *really* sure. Because, you see," she said in her most reasonable tone, "I've never seen it with my own eyes, and that's the only way to *be* sure; *isn't* it."

They just kept looking at her. She could see no way out.

"But I've *heard* about it," she said with shallow cheerfulness, "from those who *have* seen it, and I don't suppose there's any good reason to doubt them."

She looked away over them again, and for all their interest in what she was about to tell them, her eyes so changed that they turned and looked, too.

The herd, which had been moving broadside to them, was being turned away, so slowly that like the turning of stars it could not quite be seen from one moment to the next; yet soon it was moving directly away from them, and even during the little while she spoke and they all watched after it, it steadily and very noticeably diminished, and the sounds of it as well.

"It happens always about this time of year," she said quietly while they watched. "Nearly all the men and horses leave, and go into the North and the West."

"Out on the range," her son said, and by his voice she knew what enchantment the idea already held for him.

"Yes," she said, "out on the range." And trying, impossibly, to imagine the range, they were touched by the breath of grandeur.

"And then before long," she continued, "everyone has been found, and brought into one place; and then . . . what you see, happens. All of them.

"Sometimes when the wind is right," she said more quietly, "you can hear them coming long before you can see them. It isn't even like a sound, at first. It's more as if something were moving far under the ground. It makes you uneasy. You wonder, why, what in the world can *that* be! Then you remember what it is and then you can really hear it. And then finally, there they all are."

She could see this did not interest them at all.

"But where are they *going?*" one asked, a little impatiently.

"I'm coming to that," she said; and she let them wait. Then she spoke slowly but casually.

"They are on their way to a railroad."

There, she thought; that's for that look you all gave me when I said I wasn't sure. She waited for them to ask; they waited for her to explain.

"A railroad," she told them, "is great hard bars of metal lying side by side, or so they tell me, and they go on and on over the ground as far as the eye can see. And great wagons run on the metal bars on wheels, like wagon wheels but smaller, and these wheels are made of solid metal too. The wagons are much bigger than any wagon you've ever seen, as big as, big as sheds, they say, and they are pulled along on the iron bars by a terrible huge dark machine, with a loud scream."

"Big as *sheds?*" one of the calves said skeptically.

"Big *enough,* anyway," the mother said. "I told you I've never seen it myself. But those wagons are so big that several of us can get inside at once. And that's exactly what happens."

Suddenly she became very quiet, for she felt that somehow, she could not imagine just how, she had said altogether too much.

"Well, *what* happens," her son wanted to know. "What do you mean, *happens.*"

She always tried hard to be a reasonably modern mother. It was probably better, she felt, to go on, than to leave them all full of imaginings and mystification. Besides, there was really nothing at all awful about what happened . . . if only one could know *why.*

"Well," she said, "it's nothing much, really. They just — why, when they all finally *get* there, why there are all the great cars waiting in a long line, and the big dark machine is up ahead . . . smoke comes out of it they say . . . and . . . well, then, they just put us into the wagons, just as many as will fit in each wagon, and when everybody is in, why . . ." She hesitated, for again, though she couldn't be sure why, she was uneasy.

"Why then," her son said, "the train takes them away."

Hearing that word, she felt a flinching of the heart. Where had he picked it up, she wondered, and she gave him a shy and curious glance. Oh dear, she thought. I should never have even *begun* to explain. "Yes," she said, "when everybody is safely in, they slide the doors shut."

They were all silent for a little while. Then one of them asked thoughtfully, "Are they taking them somewhere they don't want to go?"

"Oh, I don't think so," the mother said. "I imagine it's very nice."

"*I* want to go," she heard her son say with ardor. "I want to go right now," he cried. "Can I, Mama? *Can* I? *Please?*" And looking into his eyes, she was overwhelmed by sadness.

"Silly thing," she said, "there'll be time enough for that when you're grown up. But what I very much hope," she went on, "is that instead of being chosen to go out on the range and to make the long journey, you will grow up to be very strong and bright so they will decide that you may stay here at home with Mother. And you, too," she added, speaking to the other little males; but she could not honestly wish this for any but her own, least of all for the eldest, strongest and most proud, for she knew how few are chosen.

She could see that what she said was not received with enthusiasm.

"But I want to go," her son said.

"Why?" she asked. "I don't think any of you realize that it's a great *honor* to be chosen to stay. A great privilege. Why, it's just the most ordinary ones are taken out onto the range. But only the very pick are chosen to stay here at home. If you want to go out on the range," she said in hurried and happy inspiration, "all you have to do is be ordinary and careless and silly. If you want to have even a chance to be chosen to stay, you have to try to be stronger and bigger and braver and brighter than anyone else, and that takes *hard work. Every day.* Do you see?" And she looked happily and hopefully from one to another. "Besides," she added, aware that they were not won over, "I'm told it's a very rough life out there, and the men are unkind.

"Don't you see," she said again; and she pretended to speak to all of them, but it was only to her son.

But he only looked at her. "Why do you want me to stay home?" he asked flatly; in their silence she knew the others were asking the same question.

"Because it's safe here," she said before she knew better; and realized she had put it in the most unfortunate way possible. "Not safe, not just that," she fumbled. "I mean . . . because here we *know* what happens, and what's going to happen, and there's never any doubt about it, never any reason to wonder, to worry. Don't you see? It's just *Home,*" and she put a smile on the word, "where we all know each other and are happy and well."

They were so merely quiet, looking back at her, that she felt they were neither won over nor alienated. Then she knew of her son that he, anyhow, was most certainly not persuaded, for he asked the question she most dreaded: "Where do they go on the train?" And hearing him, she knew that she would stop at nothing to bring that curiosity and eagerness, and that tendency toward skepticism, within safe bounds.

"Nobody knows," she said, and she added, in just the tone she knew would most sharply engage them, "Not for sure, anyway."

"What do you mean, *not for sure,*" her son cried. And the oldest, biggest calf repeated the question, his voice cracking.

The mother deliberately kept silence as she gazed out over the plain, and while she was silent they all heard the last they would ever hear of all those who were going away; one last great cry, as faint almost as a breath; the infinitesimal jabbing vituperation of the dog; the solemn muttering of the earth.

"Well," she said, after even this sound was entirely lost, "there was one who came back." Their instant, trustful eyes were too much for her. She added, "Or so they say."

They gathered a little more closely around her, for now she spoke very quietly.

"It was my great-grandmother who told me," she said. "She was told it by *her* great-grandmother, who claimed she saw it with her own eyes, though of course I can't vouch for that. Because of course I wasn't even dreamed of then; and Great-grandmother was so very, very old, you see, that you couldn't always be sure she knew quite *what* she was saying."

Now that she began to remember it more clearly, she was sorry she had committed herself to telling it.

"Yes," she said, "the story is, there was one, *just* one, who ever came back, and he told what happened on the train, and where the train went and what happened after. He told it all in a rush, they say, the last things first and every which way, but as it was finally sorted out and gotten into order by those who heard it and those they told it to, this is more or less what happened:

"He said that after the men had gotten just as many of us as they could into the car he was in, so that their sides pressed tightly together and nobody could lie down, they slid the door shut with a startling rattle and a bang, and then there was a sudden jerk, so strong they might have fallen except that they were packed so closely together, and the car began to move. But after it had moved only a little way, it stopped as suddenly as it had started, so that they all nearly fell down again. You see, they were just moving up the next car that joined on behind, to put more of us into it. He could see it all between the boards of the car, because the boards were built a little apart from each other, to let in air."

Car, her son said again to himself. Now he would never forget the word.

"He said that then, for the first time in his life, he became very badly frightened, he didn't know why. But he was sure, at that moment, that there was something dreadfully to be afraid of. The others felt this same great fear. They called out loudly to those who were being put into the car behind, and the others called back, but it was no use; those who were getting aboard were between narrow white fences and then were walking up a narrow slope and the men kept jabbing them as they do when they are in an unkind humor, and there was no way to go but on into the car. There was no way to get out of the car, either: he tried, with all his might, and he was the one nearest the door.

"After the next car behind was full, and the door was shut, the train jerked forward again, and stopped again, and they put more of us into still another car, and so on, and on, until all the starting and stopping no longer frightened anybody; it was just something uncomfortable that was never going to stop, and they began instead to realize how hungry and thirsty they were. But there was no food and no water, so they just had to put up with this; and about the time they became resigned to going without their suppers (for now it was almost dark), they heard a sudden and terrible scream which frightened them even more deeply than anything had frightened them before, and the train began to move again, and they braced their legs once more for the jolt when it would stop, but this time, instead of stopping, it began to go fast, and then even faster, so fast that the ground nearby slid past like a flooded creek and the whole country, he claimed, began to move too, turning slowly around a far mountain as if it were all one great wheel. And then there was a strange kind of disturbance inside the car, he said, or even inside his very bones. He felt as if everything in him was *falling,* as if he had been filled full of a heavy liquid that all wanted to flow one way, and all the others were leaning as he was leaning, away from this queer heaviness that was trying to pull them over, and then just as suddenly this leaning heaviness was gone and they nearly fell again before they could stop leaning against it. He could never understand what this was, but it too happened so many times that they all got used to it, just as they got used to seeing the country turn like a slow wheel, and just as they got used to the long cruel screams of the engine, and the steady iron noise beneath them which made the cold darkness so fearsome, and the hunger and the thirst and the continual standing up, and the moving on and on and on as if they would never stop."

"*Didn't* they ever stop?" one asked.

"Once in a great while," she replied. "Each time they did," she said, "he thought, Oh, now *at last! At last* we can get out and stretch our tired legs and lie down! *At last* we'll be given food and water! But they never let them out. And they never gave them food or water. They never even cleaned up under them. They had to stand in their manure and in the water they made."

"Why did the train stop?" her son asked; and with somber gratification she saw that he was taking all this very much to heart.

"He could never understand why," she said. "Sometimes men would walk up and down alongside the cars, and the more nervous and the more trustful of us would call out; but they were only looking around, they never seemed to do anything. Sometimes he could see many houses and bigger buildings together where people lived. Sometimes it was far out in the country and after they had stood still for a long time they would hear a little noise which quickly became louder, and then became suddenly a noise so loud it stopped their breathing, and during this noise something black would go by, very close, and so fast it couldn't be seen. And then it was gone as suddenly as it had appeared, and the noise became small, and then in the silence their train would start up again.

"Once, he tells us, something very strange happened. They were standing still, and cars of a very different kind began to move slowly past. These cars were not red, but black, with many glass windows like those in a house; and he says they were as full of human beings as the car he was in was full of our kind. And one of these people looked into his eyes and smiled, as if he liked him, or as if he knew only too well how hard the journey was.

"So by his account it happens to them, too," she said, with a certain pleased vindictiveness. "Only they were sitting down at their ease, not standing. And the one who smiled was eating."

She was still, trying to think of something; she couldn't quite grasp the thought.

"But didn't they *ever* let them out?" her son asked.

The oldest calf jeered. "Of *course* they did. He came back, didn't he? How would he ever come back if he didn't get out?"

"They didn't let them out," she said, "for a long, long time."

"How long?"

"So long, and he was so tired, he could never quite be sure. But he said that it turned from night to day and from day to night and back again several times over, with the train moving nearly all of this time, and that when it finally stopped, early one morning, they were all so tired and so discouraged that they hardly even noticed any longer, let alone felt any hope that anything would change for them, ever again; and then all of a sudden men came up and put up a wide walk and unbarred the door and slid it open, and it was the most wonderful and happy moment of his life when he saw the door open, and walked into the open air with all his joints trembling, and drank the water and ate the delicious food they had ready for him; it was worth the whole terrible journey."

Now that these scenes came clear before her, there was a faraway shining in her eyes, and her voice, too, had something in it of the faraway.

"When they had eaten and drunk all they could hold they lifted up their heads and looked around, and everything they saw made them happy. Even the trains made them cheerful now, for now they were no longer afraid of them. And though these trains were forever breaking to pieces and joining again with other broken pieces, with shufflings and clashings and rude cries, they hardly paid them attention any more, they were so pleased to be in their new home, and so surprised and delighted to find they were among thousands upon thousands of strangers of their own kind, all lifting up their voices in peacefulness and thanksgiving, and they were so wonderstruck by all they could see, it was so beautiful and so grand.

"For he has told us that now they lived among fences as white as bone, so many, and so spiderishly complicated, and shining so pure, that there's no use trying even to hint at the beauty and the splendor of it to anyone who knows only the pitiful little outfittings of a ranch. Beyond these mazy fences, through the dark and bright smoke which continually turned along the sunlight, dark buildings stood shoulder to shoulder in a wall as huge and proud as mountains. All through the air, all the time, there was an iron humming like the humming of the iron bar after it has been struck to tell the men it is time to eat, and in all the air, all the time, there was the same strange kind of iron strength which makes the silence before lightning so different from all other silence.

"Once for a little while the wind shifted and blew over them straight from the great buildings, and it brought a strange and very powerful smell which confused and disturbed them. He could never quite describe this smell, but he has told us it was unlike anything he had ever known before. It smelled like old fire, he said, and old blood and fear and darkness and sorrow and most terrible and brutal force and something else, something in it that made him want to run away. This sudden uneasiness and this wish to run away swept through every one of them, he tells us, so that they were all moved at once as restlessly as so many leaves in a wind, and there was great worry in their voices. But soon the leaders among them concluded that it was simply the way men must smell when there are a great many of them living together. Those dark buildings must be crowded very full of men, they decided, probably as many thousands of them, indoors, as there were of us, outdoors; so it was no wonder their smell was so strong and, to our kind, so unpleasant. Besides, it was so clear now in every other way that men were not as we had always supposed, but were doing everything they knew how to make us comfortable and happy, that we ought to just put up with their smell, which after all they couldn't help, any more than we could help our own. Very likely men didn't like the way we smelled, any more than we liked theirs. They passed along these ideas to the others, and soon everyone felt more calm, and then the wind changed again, and the fierce smell no longer came to them, and the smell of their own kind was back again, very strong of course, in such a crowd, but ever so homey and comforting, and everyone felt easy again.

"They were fed and watered so generously, and treated so well, and the majesty and the loveliness of this place where they had all come to rest was so far beyond anything they had ever known or dreamed of, that many of the simple and ignorant, whose memories were short, began to wonder whether that whole difficult journey, or even their whole lives up to now, had ever really been. Hadn't it all been just shadows, they murmured, just a bad dream?

"Even the sharp ones, who knew very well it had all really happened, began to figure that everything up to now had been made so full of pain only so that all they had come to now might seem all the sweeter and the more glorious. Some of the oldest and deepest were even of a mind that all the puzzle and tribulation of the journey had been sent us as a kind of harsh trying or proving of our worthiness; and that it was entirely fitting and proper that we could earn our way through to such rewards as these, only through suffering, and through being patient under pain which was beyond our understanding; and that now at the last, to those who had borne all things well, all things were made known: for the mystery of suffering stood revealed in joy. And now as they looked back over all that was past, all their sorrows and bewilderments seemed so little and so fleeting that, from the simplest among them even to the most wise, they could feel only the kind of amused pity we feel toward the very young when, with the first thing that hurts them or they are forbidden, they are sure there is nothing kind or fair in all creation, and carry on accordingly, raving and grieving as if their hearts would break."

She glanced among them with an indulgent smile, hoping the little lesson would sink home. They seemed interested but somewhat dazed. I'm talking way over their heads, she realized. But by now she herself was too deeply absorbed in her story to modify it much. *Let* it be, she thought, a little impatient; it's over *my* head, for that matter.

"They had hardly before this even wondered that they were alive," she went on, "and now all of a sudden they felt they understood *why* they were. This made them very happy, but they were still only beginning to enjoy this new wisdom when quite a new and different kind of restiveness ran among them. Before they quite knew it they were all moving once again, and now they realized that they were being moved, once more, by men, toward still some other place and purpose they could not know. But during these last hours they had been so well that now they felt no uneasiness, but all moved forward calm and sure toward better things still to come; he has told us that he no longer felt as if he were being driven, even as it became clear that they were going toward the shade of those great buildings; but guided.

"He was guided between fences which stood ever more and more narrowly near each other, among companions who were pressed ever more and more closely against one another; and now as he felt their warmth against him it was not uncomfortable, and his pleasure in it was not through any need to be close among others through anxiousness, but was a new kind of strong and gentle delight, at being so very close, so deeply of his own kind, that it seemed as if the very breath and heartbeat of each one were being exchanged through all that multitude, and each was another, and others were each, and each was a multitude, and the multitude was one. And quieted and made mild within this melting, they now entered the cold shadow cast by the buildings, and now with every step the smell of the buildings grew stronger, and in the darkening air the glittering of the fences was ever more queer.

"And now as they were pressed ever more intimately together he could see ahead of him a narrow gate, and he was strongly pressed upon from either side and from behind, and went in eagerly, and now he was between two fences so narrowly set that he brushed either fence with either flank, and walked alone, seeing just one other ahead of him, and knowing of just one other behind him, and for a moment the strange thought came to him, that the one ahead was his father, and that the one behind was the son he had never begotten.

"And now the light was so changed he knew he must have come inside one of the gloomy and enormous buildings, and the smell was so much stronger that it seemed almost to burn his nostrils, and the swell and the somber new light blended together and became some other thing again, beyond his describing to us except to say that the whole air beat with it like one immense heart and it was as if the beating of this heart were pure violence infinitely manifolded upon violence; so that the uneasy feeling stirred in him again that it would be wise to turn around and run out of this place just as fast and as far as ever he could go. This he heard, as if he were telling it to himself at the top of his voice, but it came from somewhere so deep and so dark inside him that he could only hear the shouting of it as less than a whisper, as just a hot and chilling breath, and he scarcely heeded it, there was so much else to attend to.

"For as he walked along in this sudden and complete loneliness, he tells us, this wonderful knowledge of being one with all his race meant less and less to him, and in its place came something still more wonderful; he knew what it was to be himself alone, a creature separate and different from any other, who had never been before, and would never be again. He could feel this in his whole weight as he walked, and in each foot as he put it down and gave his weight to it and moved about it, and in every muscle as he moved, and it was a pride which lifted him up and made him feel large, and a pleasure which pierced him through. And as he began with such wondering delight to be aware of his own exact singleness in this world, he also began to understand (or so he thought) just why these fences were set so very narrow, and just why he was walking all by himself. It stole over him, he tells us, like the feeling of a slow cool wind, that he was being guided toward some still more wonderful reward or revealing, up ahead, which he could not of course imagine, but he was sure it was being held in store for him alone.

"Just then the one ahead of him fell down with a great sigh, and was so quickly taken out of the way that he did not even have to shift the order of his hooves as he walked on. The sudden fall and the sound of that sigh dismayed him, though, and something within him told him that it would be wise to look up: and there he saw Him.

"A little bridge ran crosswise above the fences. He stood on this bridge with His feet as wide apart as He could set them. He wore spattered trousers but from the belt up He was naked and as wet as rain. Both arms were raised high above His head and in both hands He held an enormous Hammer. With a grunt which was hardly like the voice of a human being, and with all His strength, He brought this Hammer down into the forehead of our friend: who, in a blinding blazing, heard from his own mouth the beginning of a gasping sigh; then there was only darkness."

Oh, this is *enough!* it's *enough!* she cried out within herself, seeing their terrible young eyes. How *could* she have been so foolish as to tell so much!

"What happened then?" she heard, in the voice of the oldest calf, and she was horrified. This shining in their eyes: was it only excitement? no pity? no fear?

"What happened?" two others asked.

Very well, she said to herself. I've gone so far; now I'll go the rest of the way. She decided not to soften it, either. She'd teach them a lesson they wouldn't forget in a hurry.

"Very well," she was surprised to hear herself say aloud.

"How long he lay in this darkness he couldn't know, but when he began to come out of it, all he knew was the most unspeakably dreadful pain. He was upside down and very slowly swinging and turning, for he was hanging by the tendons of his heels from great frightful hooks, and he has told us that the feeling was as if his hide were being torn from him inch by inch, in one piece. And then as he became more clearly aware he found that this was exactly what was happening. Knives would sliver and slice along both flanks, between the hide and the living flesh; then there was a moment of most precious relief; then red hands seized his hide and there was a jerking of the hide and a tearing of tissue which it was almost as terrible to hear as to feel, turning his whole body and the poor head at the bottom of it; and then the knives again.

"It was so far beyond anything he had ever known unnatural and amazing that he hung there through several more such slicings and jerkings and tearings before he was fully able to take it all in: then, with a scream, and a supreme straining of all his strength, he tore himself from the hooks and collapsed sprawling to the floor and, scrambling right to his feet, charged the men with the knives. For just a moment they were so astonished and so terrified they could not move. Then they moved faster than he had ever known men could – and so did all the other men who chanced to be in his way. He ran down a glowing floor of blood and down endless corridors which were hung with the bleeding carcasses of our kind and with bleeding fragments of carcasses, among blood-clothed men who carried bleeding weapons, and out of that vast room into the open, and over and through one fence after another, shoving aside many an astounded stranger and shouting out warnings as he ran, and away up the railroad toward the West.

"How he ever managed to get away, and how he ever found his way home, we can only try to guess. It's told that he scarcely knew, himself, by the time he came to this part of his story. He was impatient with those who interrupted him to ask about that, he had so much more important things to tell them, and by then he was so exhausted and so far gone that he could say nothing very clear about the little he did know. But we can realize that he must have had really tremendous strength, otherwise he couldn't have outlived the Hammer; and that strength such as his – which we simply don't see these days, it's of the olden time – is capable of things our own strongest and bravest would sicken to dream of. But there was something even stronger than his strength. There was his righteous fury, which nothing could stand up against, which brought him out of that fearful place. And there was his high and burning and heroic purpose, to keep him safe along the way, and to guide him home, and to keep the breath of life in him until he could warn us. He did manage to tell us that he just followed the railroad, but how he chose one among the many which branched out from that place, he couldn't say. He told us, too, that from time to time he recognized shapes of mountains and other landmarks, from his journey by train, all reappearing backward and with a changed look and hard to see, too (for he was shrewd enough to travel mostly at night), but still recognizable. But that isn't enough to account for it. For he has told us, too, that he simply *knew* the way; that he didn't hesitate one moment in choosing the right line of railroad, or even think of it as choosing; and that the landmarks didn't really guide him, but just made him the more sure of what he was already sure of; and that whenever he *did* encounter human beings — and during the later stages of his journey, when he began to doubt he would live to tell us, he traveled day and night — they never so much as moved to make him trouble, but stopped dead in their tracks, and their jaws fell open.

"And surely we can't wonder that their jaws fell open. I'm sure yours would, if you had seen him as he arrived, and I'm very glad I wasn't there to see it, either, even though it is said to be the greatest and most momentous day of all the days that ever were or shall be. For we have the testimony of eyewitnesses, how he looked, and it is only too vivid, even to hear of. He came up out of the East as much staggering as galloping (for by now he was so worn out by pain and exertion and loss of blood that he could hardly stay upright), and his heels were so piteously torn by the hooks that his hooves doubled under more often than not, and in his broken forehead the mark of the Hammer was like the socket for a third eye.

"He came to the meadow where the great trees made shade over the water. 'Bring them all together!' he cried out, as soon as he could find breath. 'All!' Then he drank; and then he began to speak to those who were already there; for as soon as he saw himself in the water it was as clear to him as it was to those who watched him that there was no time left to send for the others. His hide was all gone from his head and his neck and his forelegs and his chest and most of one side and a part of the other side. It was flung backward from his naked muscles by the wind of his running and now it lay around him in the dust like a ragged garment. They say there is no imagining how terrible and in some way how grand the eyeball is when the skin has been taken entirely from around it; his eyes, which were bare in this way, also burned with pain, and with the final energies of his life, and with his desperate concern to warn us while he could; and he rolled his eyes wildly while he talked, or looked piercingly from one to another of the listeners, interrupting himself to cry out, '*Believe* me! Oh, *believe* me!' For it had evidently never occurred to him that he might not be believed, and must make this last great effort, in addition to all he had gone through for us, to *make* himself believed; so that he groaned with sorrow and with rage and railed at them without tact or mercy for their slowness to believe. He had scarcely what you could call a voice left, but with this relic of a voice he shouted and bellowed and bullied us and insulted us, in the agony of his concern. While he talked he bled from the mouth, and the mingled blood and saliva hung from his chin like the beard of a goat.

"Some say that with his naked face, and his savage eyes, and that beard and the hide lying off his bare shoulders like shabby clothing, he looked almost human. But others feel this is an irreverence even to think; and others, that it is a poor compliment to pay the one who told us, at such cost to himself, the true ultimate purpose of Man. Some did not believe he had ever come from our ranch in the first place, and of course he was so different from us in appearance and even in his voice, and so changed from what he might ever have looked or sounded like before, that nobody could recognize him for sure, though some were sure they did. Others suspected that he had been sent among us with his story for some mischievous and cruel purpose, and the fact that they could not imagine what this purpose might be, made them, naturally, all the more suspicious. Some believed he was actually a man, trying — and none too successfully, they said — to disguise himself as one of us; and again the fact that they could not imagine why a man would do this, made them all the more uneasy. There were quite a few who doubted that anyone who could get into such bad condition as he was in, was fit even to give reliable information, let alone advice, to those in good health. And some whispered, even while he spoke, that he had turned lunatic; and many came to believe this. It wasn't only that his story was so fantastic; there was good reason to wonder, many felt, whether anybody in his right mind would go to such trouble for others. But even those who did not believe him listened intently, out of curiosity to hear so wild a tale, and out of the respect it is only proper to show any creature who is in the last agony.

"What he told, was what I have just told you. But his purpose was away beyond just the telling. When they asked questions, no matter how curious or suspicious or idle or foolish, he learned, toward the last, to answer them with all the patience he could and in all the detail he could remember. He even invited them to examine his wounded heels and the pulsing wound in his head as closely as they pleased. He even begged them to, for he knew that before everything else, he must be believed. For unless we could believe him, wherever could we find any reason, or enough courage, to do the hard and dreadful things he told us we must do!

"It was only these things, he cared about. Only for these, he came back."

Now clearly remembering what these things were, she felt her whole being quail. She looked at the young ones quickly and as quickly looked away.

"While he talked," she went on, "and our ancestors listened, men came quietly among us; one of them shot him. Whether he was shot in kindness or to silence him is an endlessly disputed question which will probably never be settled. Whether, even, he died of the shot, or through his own great pain and weariness (for his eyes, they say, were glazing for some time before the men came), we will never be sure. Some suppose even that he may have died of his sorrow and his concern for us. Others feel that he had quite enough to die of, without that. All these things are tangled and lost in the disputes of those who love to theorize and to argue. There is no arguing about his dying words, though; they were very clearly remembered:

"Tell them! Believe!"

After a while her son asked, "What did he tell them to do?"

She avoided his eyes. "There's a great deal of disagreement about that, too," she said after a moment. "You see, he was so very tired."

They were silent.

"So tired," she said, "some think that toward the end, he really *must* have been out of his mind."

"Why?" asked her son.

"Because he was so tired out and so badly hurt."

They looked at her mistrustfully.

"And because of what he told us to do."

"What did he tell us to do?" he son asked again.

Her throat felt dry. "Just . . . things you can hardly bear even to think of. That's all."

They waited. "Well, *what?*" her son asked in a cold, accusing voice.

"*'Each one is himself,'*" she said shyly. "*'Not of the herd. Himself alone.'* That's one."

"What else?"

"*'Obey nobody. Depend on none.'*"

"What else?"

She found that she was moved. "*'Break down the fences,'*" she said less shyly. "*'Tell everybody, everywhere.'*"

"Where?"

"Everywhere. You see, he thought there must be ever so many more of us than we had ever known."

They were silent. "What else?" her son asked.

"*'For if even a few do not hear me, or disbelieve me, we are all betrayed.'*"

"Betrayed?"

"He meant, doing as men want us to. Not for ourselves, or the good of each other."

They were puzzled.

"Because, you see, he felt there was no other way." Again her voice altered: " '*All who are put on the range are put onto trains. All who are put onto trains meet the Man With The Hammer. All who stay home are kept there to breed others to go onto the range, and so betray themselves and their kind and their children forever.*

" '*We are brought into this life only to be victims; and there is no other way for us unless we save ourselves.*'

"Do you understand?"

Still they were puzzled, she saw; and no wonder, poor things. But now the ancient lines rang in her memory, terrible and brave. They made her somehow proud. She began actually to want to say them.

" '*Never be taken,*' " she said. " '*Never be driven. Let those who can, kill Man. Let those who cannot, avoid him.*' "

She looked around at them.

"What else?" her son asked, and in his voice there was a rising valor.

She looked straight into his eyes. " '*Kill the yearlings,*' " she said very gently. " '*Kill the calves.*' "

She saw the valor leave his eyes.

"Kill us?"

She nodded, " '*So long as Man holds dominion over us,*' " she said. And in dread and amazement she heard herself add, " '*Bear no young.*' "

With this they all looked at her at once in such a way that she loved her child, and all these others, as never before; and there dilated within her such a sorrowful and marveling grandeur that for a moment she was nothing except her own inward whisper, "Why, *I* am one alone. And of the herd, too. Both at once. All one."

Her son's voice brought her back: "Did they do what he told them to?"

The oldest one scoffed, "Would we be here, if they had?"

"They say some did," the mother replied. "Some tried. Not all."

"What did the men do to them?" another asked.

"I don't know," she said. "It was such a very long time ago."

"Do you believe it?" asked the oldest calf.

"There are some who believe it," she said.

"Do *you?*"

"I'm told that far back in the wildest corners of the range there are some of us, mostly very, very old ones, who have never been taken. It's said that they meet, every so often, to talk and just to think together about the heroism and the terror of two sublime Beings, The One Who

Came Back, and The Man With The Hammer. Even here at home, some of the old ones, and some of us who are just old-fashioned, believe it, or parts of it anyway. I know there are some who say that a hollow at the center of the forehead – a sort of shadow of the Hammer's blow – is a sign of very special ability. And I remember how Great-grandmother used to sing an old, pious song, let's see now, yes, 'Be not like dumb-driven cattle, be a hero in the strife.' But there aren't many. Not any more."

"Do *you* believe it?" the oldest calf insisted; and now she was touched to realize that every one of them, from the oldest to the youngest, needed very badly to be sure about that.

"Of course not, silly," she said; and all at once she was overcome by a most curious shyness, for it occurred to her that in the course of time, this young thing might be bred to her. "It's just an old, old legend." With a tender little laugh she added, lightly, "We use it to frighten children with."

By now the light was long on the plain and the herd was only a fume of gold near the horizon. Behind it, dung steamed, and dust sank gently to the shattered ground. She looked far away for a moment, wondering. Something – it was like a forgotten word on the tip of the tongue. She felt the sudden chill of the late afternoon and she wondered what she had been wondering about. "Come, children," she said briskly, "it's high time for supper." And she turned away; they followed.

The trouble was, her son was thinking, you could never trust her. If she said a thing was so, she was probably just trying to get her way with you. If she said a thing wasn't so, it probably was so. But you never could be sure. Not without seeing for yourself. I'm going to go, he told himself; I don't care *what* she wants. And if it isn't so, why then I'll live on the range and make the great journey and find out what *is* so. And if what she told was true, why then I'll know ahead of time and the one *I* will charge is The Man With The Hammer. I'll put Him and His Hammer out of the way forever, and that will make me an even better hero than The One Who Came Back.

So, when the mother glanced at him in concern, not quite daring to ask her question, he gave her his most docile smile, and snuggled his head against her, and she was comforted.

The littlest and youngest of them was doing double skips in his efforts to keep up with her. Now that he wouldn't be interrupting her, and none of the big ones would hear and make fun of him, he shyly whispered his question, so warmly moistly ticklish that she felt as if he were licking her ear.

"What is it, darling?" she asked, bending down.

"What's a train?"

1. Why is the mother reluctant to tell the tale? What impels her to tell it anyway?
2. Does she really believe it is true, or not? Are there varying degrees of belief? What makes her not want to believe?
3. Can you think of any cases in which people around you deny plain evidence and substitute comfortable fictions?
4. What, if anything, do you think Agee is saying about the meaning of life?
5. Why do you think Agee decided to tell a story about cattle rather than, say, a story about a human "One Who Came Back"? Does this help him to make his point better? How?
6. What *is* the point of the story?

Was a Man

PHILIP BOOTH

Was a man, was a two-
faced man, pretended
he wasn't who he was,
who, in a men's room,
faced his hung-over
face in a mirror hung
over the towel rack.
The mirror was cracked.
Shaving close in that
looking glass, he nicked
his throat, bled blue
blood, grabbed a new
towel to patch the wrong
scratch, knocked off
the mirror and, facing
himself, almost intact,
in final terror hung
the wrong face back.

---

1. What actually happens to the man in the poem? Follow the action through, putting it in other words so that it is clear in your mind.
2. Have you ever known a "two-faced man"? In what ways did he pretend "he wasn't who he was"? Be specific.
3. Why does the man bleed *blue* blood?

4. Why does accidentally facing himself cause terror? Do you know anyone who is afraid to face something about himself. How does he avoid facing it?
5. How can you avoid the fate of the two-faced man? Give specific examples of situations in which there is a temptation not to be yourself.
6. Can you think of any examples of two-faced people in the readings from this book?

---

1. The subject of a girl looking into a mirror is a common one in painting, but the act of looking into a mirror may have a number of different meanings. We have seen one in Philip Booth's "Was a Man." What do you think Picasso's meaning is? What does the girl see in the mirror?
2. Picasso uses a semi-abstract technique for making his point (or points). What advantage does this give him?
3. What are some other ways one might look at himself in a mirror? (See "Morning Song" from *Senlin* in Unit 5, for example.)

PLATE XIV

GIRL BEFORE A MIRROR: Pablo Picasso Collection, The Museum of Modern Art, New York; gift of Mrs. Simon Guggenheim

Index of Authors and Titles

"A & P," John Updike, pp. 139–44
"A Dream of Fair Women," Kingsley Amis, pp. 50–51
"A Mother's Tale," James Agee, pp. 203–19
"A Study of Two Pears," Wallace Stevens, p. 11
Agee, James, "A Mother's Tale," pp. 203–19
Aiken, Conrad, "Morning Song" from *Senlin,* pp. 62–63
Amis, Kingsley, "A Dream of Fair Women," pp. 50–51
"Arrangement in Black and White," Dorothy Parker, pp. 33–36
Auden, W. H., "The Unknown Citizen," p. 167
Baldwin, James, "Sonny's Blues," pp. 105–31
"Big Two-Hearted River: Part II," Ernest Hemingway, pp. 17–25
Booth, Philip, "Was a Man," p. 221
Bradbury, Ray, "The Death of Colonel Freeleigh," pp. 57–61
Coffin, Robert P. Tristram, "Grinding Scythe," pp. 194–96
Ellison, Ralph, from *Invisible Man,* pp. 154–66
"Ex-Basketball Player," John Updike, p. 79
Forster, E. M., "My Wood," pp. 85–88
"Grinding Scythe," Robert P. Tristram Coffin, pp. 194–96
Gunn, Thom, "Innocence," p. 98
Hemingway, Ernest, "Big Two-Hearted River: Part II," pp. 17–25
"Innocence," Thom Gunn, p. 98
from *Invisible Man,* Ralph Ellison, pp. 154–66
Jarrell, Randall, "The Death of the Ball Turret Gunner," p. 179

Kazin, Alfred, "The Human Factory," pp. 173–78
Lawrence, D. H., "Snake," pp. 37–38
"Memories of a Missouri Farm," Mark Twain, pp. 185–93
"Morning Song," from *Senlin,* Conrad Aiken, pp. 62–63
Morris, Wright, from *The Ram in the Thicket,* pp. 72–78
"Mr. Flood's Party," Edwin Arlington Robinson, pp. 132–33
"My Wood," E. M. Forster, pp. 85–88
Parker, Dorothy, "Arrangement in Black and White," pp. 33–36
Porter, Katherine Anne, "The Witness," pp. 94–97
Pound, Ezra, "Salutation," p. 89
Robinson, Edwin Arlington, "Mr. Flood's Party," pp. 132–33
"Salutation," Ezra Pound, p. 89
"Snake,"D. H. Lawrence, pp. 37–38
"Sonny's Blues," James Baldwin, pp. 105–31
Stevens, Wallace, "A Study of Two Pears," p. 11
"The Death of Colonel Freeleigh," Ray Bradbury, pp. 57–61
"The Death of the Ball Turret Gunner," Randall Jarrell, p. 179
"The Great Figure," William Carlos Williams, p. 27
"The Human Factory," Alfred Kazin, pp. 173–78
from *The Ram in the Thicket,* Wright Morris, pp. 72–78
"The Second Tree from the Corner," E. B. White, pp. 45–49
"The Unknown Citizen," W. H. Auden, p. 167
"The Witness," Katherine Anne Porter, pp. 95–97
"Tract," William Carlos Williams, pp. 145–46
Twain, Mark, "Memories of a Missouri Farm," pp. 185–93
Updike, John, "A & P," pp. 139–44
Updike, John, "Ex-Basketball Player," p. 79
"Was A Man," Philip Booth, p. 221
White, E. B., "The Second Tree from the Corner," pp. 45–49
Williams, William Carlos, "The Great Figure," p. 27
Williams, William Carlos, "Tract," pp. 145–46

Index of Artists and Plates

American Gothic, Grant Wood, p. 81
Blind Bird, Morris Graves, p. 53
Bohrod, Aaron, *Family Tree,* p. 199
Brancusi, Constantin, *The Kiss,* p. 149
Demuth, Charles, *I Saw the Figure 5 in Gold,* p. 29
Echo of a Scream, David Alfaro Siqueiros, p. 181
Family Tree, Aaron Bohrod, p. 199
Girl Before a Mirror, Pablo Picasso, p. 223
Government Bureau, George Tooker, p. 169
Goya, Francisco, *The Prisoner,* p. 135
Graves, Morris, *Blind Bird,* p. 53
Grosz, George, *Heilige Nacht,* p. 101
Heilige Nacht, George Grosz, p. 101
I Saw the Figure 5 in Gold, Charles Demuth, p. 29
Kalf, Willem, *Still Life,* p. 13
Picasso, Pablo, *Girl Before a Mirror,* p. 223
Rauschenberg, Robert, *Reservoir,* p. 41
Reservoir, Robert Rauschenberg, p. 41
Siqueiros, David Alfaro, *Echo of a Scream,* p. 181
Still Life, Willem Kalf, p. 13
The Kiss, Constantin Brancusi, p. 149
The Money Changer and His Wife, Marinus van Roijmerswaele, p. 91
The Prisoner, Francisco Goya, p. 135

The Starry Night, Vincent van Gogh, p. 65
Tooker, George, *Government Bureau,* p. 169
van Gogh, Vincent, *The Starry Night,* p. 65
van Roijmerswaele, Marinus, *The Money Changer and His Wife,* p. 91
Wood, Grant, *American Gothic,* p. 81

P 5
Q 6
R 7
S 8